T0162469

Praise for The Interfaith Family Journal

"Susan Katz Miller is a pioneer on multi-religious belonging and our wise guide in the realm of non-binary faith. Miller's comprehensive yet accessible blueprint empowers interfaith families and individuals in preserving, sustaining, and growing complex, beautiful religious and spiritual identities in the modern world. *The Interfaith Family Journal* is the gold standard map on this path."

—J. Dana Trent, professor of world religions and author of *Saffron Cross:
The Unlikely Story of a How a Christian Minister Married a Hindu Monk*

"Susan Katz Miller has created a glorious and indispensable workbook for interfaith families navigating their collective spiritual life. She guides family partners through a series of smart journaling exercises that will help them see what would nourish them most thoroughly in the spiritual dimension and how to change and grow gracefully in that path. As someone who writes and teaches about how to create powerful personal and family rituals, I'm deeply impressed with the way she emphasizes tradition and helps families assess how to amplify and expand their own. She gets to this by explicit questions like: 'On which religious or secular holidays would you expect to exchange gifts in your household?' This journal is a flexible tool and true treasure for multi-faith families of all varieties."

—Meg Cox, author of *The Book of New Family Traditions:
How to Create Great Rituals for Holidays & Every Day*

"No need to worry about having a difficult or painful conversation that goes in circles. Rather, the activities in Susan Katz Miller's *The Interfaith Family Journal* will assist you to plan and dream together, with resources to help you deepen your connection as you go. As a couples and family therapist, I will be recommending this vital resource to all my interfaith clients and their families."

—Jennifer Kogan, MSW, LICSW

"Susan Katz Miller has created a way for interfaith families to embark on a joyful journey of discovery. As part of an interfaith family for more than twenty-five years, (Muslim, Jewish, Unitarian Universalist) I know that stories of family histories are crucial to understanding who we are today. This journal will become a part of your family's story for many years to come."

—Aisha Hauser, MSW

"A brilliantly original, practical approach to interfaith family building that combines structure with flexibility, common sense with spiritual depth. This book will become a lifelong companion."

—M.H.P. Rosenbaum, co-author, *Celebrating Our Differences: Living Two Faiths in One Marriage*;
Director, Dovetail Institute for Interfaith Family Resources

"Having spent my rabbinate working to support interfaith couples, I can think of no better gift than a tangible way to communicate about how to navigate two different backgrounds in one home. This will be an invaluable resource for clergy and wedding officiants and a beautiful resource to offer so many couples before their wedding and as they begin their marriage."

—Rabbi Ari Moffic, founder of Cohere

"*The Interfaith Family Journal* is a wonderfully inventive and engaging resource for families blessed with more than a single faith tradition. More than this, its value reaches far beyond the 'interfaith' issue. It is a tool for clarifying a family's aims for religious, spiritual, and cultural meaning in their lives—and helping a family to tailor its life accordingly. It is pitch perfect for *all* twenty-first-century families."

—Sheila C. Gordon, PhD, President and Founder, Interfaith Community, Inc.

"As the child of an interfaith family, partner in an interfaith marriage, and co-director of an interfaith arts community, I've found that most questions of difference are to be lived rather than solved. In this guide, Susan Katz Miller equips us with creative tools and courageous tactics to do just that."

—Rev. Erik W. Martínez Resly, Founder and Co-Director, The Sanctuaries

The Interfaith Family Journal

The Interfaith Family Journal

Susan Katz Miller

Skinner House Books
Boston

Copyright © 2019 by the Unitarian Universalist Association. All rights reserved. Published by Skinner House Books, an imprint of the Unitarian Universalist Association, a liberal religious organization with more than 1,000 congregations in the U.S. and Canada, 24 Farnsworth St., Boston, MA 02210–1409.

www.skinnerhouse.org

Printed in the United States

Cover and text design by Suzanne Morgan
Author photo by Stephanie Williams, Stephaniewilliamsimages.com

print ISBN: 978-1-55896-825-7

6 5 4 3 2 1
23 22 21 20 19

Library of Congress Cataloging-in-Publication Data
Names: Miller, Susan Katz, author.
Title: The interfaith family journal / Susan Katz Miller.
Description: Boston : Skinner House Books, [2019]
Identifiers: LCCN 2018048544 | ISBN 9781558968257 (pbk.)
Subjects: LCSH: Families--Religious life.
Classification: LCC BL625.6 .M56 2019 | DDC 204/.41--dc23
LC record available at https://lccn.loc.gov/2018048544

CONTENTS

INTRODUCTION

I come from a great, big, three-generation interfaith family. Our Thanksgiving features about sixty family members—Jews, Protestants, Catholics, Quakers, Buddhists, and atheists. Together, my parents, siblings, cousins, aunts, and uncles represent many different interfaith family choices and paths. Some celebrate one religion. Some draw on two or more. Some lead strictly secular lives. And we continue to get together on a regular basis to express our love and revel in our connection to each other.

Interfaith families are a growing and important segment of society. One in every five Americans now grows up in an interfaith family, according to a recent study by the Pew Research Center. Given this reality, this journal is not going to defend the formation or existence of interfaith families—we're already here! Instead, these pages will help you to find a way of living inside our whirling religious kaleidoscope without getting overwhelmed. The exercises here will support you in finding your own way to build the bonds of love while honoring more than one culture, more than one set of traditions, and more than one set of beliefs, in a way that will create joy and empowerment. It will bring you through a process of discerning your own best path as an interfaith family—a process that can itself provide intellectual and spiritual nourishment.

Is this journal meant for my family?

An interfaith family can include any two religions, or more than two religions, or a religious/non-religious relationship, or atheists from different religious backgrounds. Your family might share a broad religious label, but include both secular Jews and Orthodox Jews. Or it might include members from two very different Protestant denominations, or Buddhists from different cultural traditions. While not technically interfaith, these families may still find this journal tremendously helpful. On a philosophical level, all families are interfaith families because no two individuals have identical cultures, traditions, practices, or beliefs, even when they share a single religious affiliation. So this journal could actually help any family. For those who are struggling to figure out how to make it all work, or are just unsure of the options, going through this journal process could be transformative.

You may not think of your family as interfaith, or you may dislike the term. The terminology is imperfect! Some people prefer *multifaith* because their family includes three or more religions. But I like the sense that "inter" implies active engagement, rather than simple co-existence. Some people prefer *interreligious,* because while *faith* can be a synonym for belief-centric religions including Christianity and Islam, it is less appropriate for describing more practice-based religious cultures, including Judaism, Buddhism, and Hinduism. And families with one or more atheist, secular humanist, or agnostic member have argued for new terminology to replace *interfaith*, including *interbelief, intercultural*, or *interworldview.* While acknowledging this linguistic flux, this journal uses the term *interfaith* because the intention is to reach and include the greatest number of families searching for help. But also, I admit to sticking with *interfaith* as the historical term of art, because I feel harmonic resonance with the positive linguistic echoes of other words that use the prefix *inter-*, including *interest, intertwine,* and *intercourse.*

So, which is the best path?

A lot of books urge interfaith families to choose a particular path, or to avoid certain paths. Those books tell us how we should practice, where we should affiliate, and what we should or should not do to educate our interfaith children. Many of those books have been written by religious leaders, people funded by institutions with agendas, or people who did not grow up in interfaith families themselves.

This journal is different because it proposes that there is no one path that is going to work for every interfaith family, and that each family must make its own decisions. It assumes that you do not necessarily have to choose one religion, or both religions, or many religions, or no religions in order to be a functional interfaith family. The questions and exercises here will help you to anticipate the challenges of being an interfaith family, no matter which path you are on.

This journal is also different because it begins with the assumption that interfaith families, so often characterized as problematic, can actually be inspiring and successful. It will help you to build a sacred circle around your family, and articulate a boundary to separate the life you are choosing together from any negative or doubting voices in broader society. It will help you to infuse your interfaith family with creativity and pleasure. And it will help you to see your interfaith family as a catalyst for compassion and peace.

Is this journal neutral or does it have an angle?

It is true that everyone brings their own experiences to the interfaith family discussion. Everyone has biases. But because I grew up in a complex interfaith family, I approach this topic through multiple lenses, rather than from a single religious viewpoint. I am the daughter of a Jewish and a Protestant parent. I am married to a Protestant. I was raised in Reform Judaism. I spent years living in a predominantly Muslim country with strong indigenous African traditions, and then years living in a predominantly Catholic country with African religious influences and strong indigenous traditions of the Americas. I have a sibling raising Jewish kids and a sibling raising Catholic kids. My family tree includes Buddhist and atheist family members, and both Jewish and Protestant clergy members. And my own children grew up in an independent interfaith family community with education in both Judaism and Christianity, as described in my book *Being Both: Embracing Two Religions in One Interfaith Family*.

Professionally, I have been helping interfaith families for more than a decade, through my book, my blog, workshops, conferences, coaching sessions, and through work with a vast array of theologians and clergy, including academics, rabbis, priests, and ministers, as well as Muslims, Hindus, Sikhs, and humanist leaders. Finally, this book is published by a Unitarian Universalist press. So, while no one can be completely neutral in discussing interfaith family choices, I bring an unusually broad variety of influences and experiences to this book. My agenda is simply to help every interfaith family find the type of support, practices, and community that they want and deserve.

While many previous books on interfaith families have assumed an audience of Christian and Jewish heterosexual couples, this journal consciously strives to decenter white Christian heteronormativity, and to work for people and families representing any number of religions and identities. The idea here is to serve the growing number of interfaith families, whether Muslim/Jewish/Buddhist, Hindu/Sikh, or Pagan/Unitarian Universalist/atheist. There are other resources (some of them listed in the Resources section at the back of the journal) more specific to the issue of, say, celebrating Christmas and Hanukkah. In contrast, the questions here do not refer specifically to, for instance, the role of Jesus, although Jesus may play a role in your responses and discussions. Instead, this journal can help any family recognize and articulate their own specific religious differences and learn how to live with them, rather than reconciling personal theologies.

How exactly will this journal help?

The questions, exercises, and activities here are designed to support you in taking control of your own interfaith family narrative. Whether your family is Jewish and Hindu, Catholic and atheist, Muslim and Baptist, Buddhist and Pagan, or represents three or more religions, using this journal will stimulate the deep reflection and honest discussion necessary to plan and create a life that works for you.

In these pages, you will consider questions that may at times push you into uncomfortable conversations. What do you believe? Which rituals and holidays and values are most meaningful to you? How do you feel about the beliefs and traditions of the other members of your family? How can your family find or create a community where you feel comfortable? If you have children, how will you communicate to them what is most important to you and to your partner?

The very process of wrestling with these questions can forge intellectual, spiritual, and creative bonds. Through this process, you may come to feel closer to your family members, across the generations. And you will feel the satisfaction of deeper understanding and intimate communication on essential and existential questions.

This journal may often seem to emphasize how we *do* religion more than what we *believe*. Differences in religious belief systems are important, and it may be useful to find clergy to discuss these with you in depth, if belief differences are a challenge in your relationship. But for many families, figuring out the logistics of how to practice and celebrate together is a powerful process, often revealing our beliefs and helping us to discuss them with each other.

By the time you finish this journal, you may decide to choose one family religion, or more than one, or no religion, or all religions, or some combination of the above. Or you may decide that you do not need to decide right now. Each of these paths will have distinct benefits and challenges. Your decision-making process will depend on many variables, including your own beliefs and traditions and cultures; those of your partner or intimate family members; the presence and influence of parents or other family members; and the support of mentors, clergy, and communities in your geographic area. No one else can tell you the right path for your family: You must do the work to figure it out together.

After we do this journal, will it all be settled?

Choosing a path for your interfaith family at the outset of your relationship does not mean your work is done. You will also need the confidence and flexibility to make the necessary adjustments to your plan as you go along. That may mean returning to this journal months or years later to work through some of the sections again together, or perhaps with a new partner or family member.

For instance, for the first twenty-five years of my marriage, I did not belong to a synagogue, but now I do. At the same time, I am far more comfortable in churches (and mosques) than I was when I got married. In fact, more than once in recent years, I have found myself speaking from the pulpit at a church service. After a rabbi and a minister co-officiated at our wedding, I did not think

I would ever need a rabbi or a minister in my life again. Now, I am very pleased to have close relationships with multiple rabbis and ministers who support my family. And on top of all of this, my attachment to my interfaith identity, as something distinct and valuable, has only grown over time.

None of us are fixed in our religious, spiritual, cultural, or philosophical orientations, or the way we do or do not want to practice. We change over time, in relation to each other, and in relation to the people, ideas, and practices we encounter in the world around us. People convert, people begin celebrating more than one religion simultaneously, people leave religion altogether. Children mature and begin to express their own opinions, sometimes inspiring a reconfiguration of the way an interfaith family celebrates. According to the Pew Research Center, religious and cultural identities in America are increasingly fluid and flexible, even outside the context of interfaith families. So while you may have married years ago, or you may have children who are half-grown, it is never too late to take the time to work through this journal together, to find the best way forward together. And it is never too late to improve your interfaith literacy, whether or not you are a religious practitioner.

So how does this journal work?

This journal is designed to engage two or more adults in working together. The collaborative process will prompt you to articulate your experiences and feelings in ways that will help you clarify your own thoughts and emotions. So your first step will be to figure out who will go through this process with you and become your "journal partner."

For many, the journal partner will be a romantic partner, whether you are dating, engaged, married, or life partners. If you are divorced, separated, or co-parenting with someone who is not a romantic partner, a commitment to do this process together may help you choose ways to address religion with the children you share. Your journal partner could be a sperm donor or birth parent with whom you have a co-parenting arrangement. For some single parents, including widows or widowers, you may want to identify your primary support in questions of religion and culture and ask them to become your journal partner. This partner could be your parent or sibling, or a beloved friend or mentor.

For instance, if you are a single parent with an adopted child born into another culture with another religion and want your child to learn about that culture, you might find a mentor from that culture or religion to partner with you in this process. And if your child is old enough to be interested in participating, you could invite them to be part of the process by giving them their own copy of the journal and working through the exercises with them. Note that this journal will refer to the adults (or older children) participating in the process with you as your "journal partner," or just "partner."

How long will it take?

The journal guides a five-week process. In Week One, you will reflect on your experiences in childhood and adulthood, and contemplate what these experiences mean to you today. In Week Two, you will move on to thinking about whether, how, and why you want to bring these traditions forward with you into your interfaith family. In Week Three, you will figure out which local community or communities can best support the vision you are building together. In Week Four, you will work on how to mark life transitions in your interfaith family: birth, coming of age, marriage, and death. And in Week Five, you will take everything you have discovered so far and figure out how to include your parents, grandparents, siblings, and the rest of your family on the path you have chosen.

Provide each partner with their own copy of the journal. Recording your thoughts in the journal, rather than on a computer, means you end up with a keepsake, though some people may prefer electronic files (just make sure to print them out for safekeeping!). You will then set aside time to meet and discuss each chapter together, after filling out your own questionnaires separately each week. This will mean five consecutive discussions, ideally spaced a week apart.

In a hurry? You could compress the schedule and go through a chapter each day, or even work through the journal intensively in a weekend retreat together. But spacing out the chapters will give you more time to reflect on your responses, to talk to family members if your memory needs jogging, to read the responses of your journal partner carefully, to do the Interactive Exercises and Get Creative sections from each chapter together, and to absorb your thoughts about the previous week's discussion before moving on.

Here's a suggested format for making the most of each chapter. Consider putting aside one hour for each of these steps:

1. **Write.** If you can, set aside an hour to answer the numbered questions at the beginning of each chapter alone, rather than sitting together, so that you won't be distracted thinking about the reaction of your partner as you write.

2. **Read.** Next, exchange journals and read what your partner wrote, in a quiet place without interruption. Rather than jumping into a mental debate or anticipated negotiation while you are reading, try to concentrate on hearing what your partner is saying and putting yourself in their shoes.

3. **Discuss.** Come together in a quiet space to do the Interactive Exercises at the end of the chapter. If you hit a rough patch, try backing up and rereading what your partner has written, without rebutting as you read. Some exercises may only take a minute, and some you could skip altogether if they raise a topic that you have already worked out between you. Others may take up to an hour to process together.

4. **Create.** The Get Creative activities for each week are designed to help you see your interfaith family as an art collaborative: weaving together treasures and experiencing the joy of synergy. If you keep your hands busy and your brain engaged while working on these projects, you naturally create a lighter and more collaborative mood. And most of these activities are designed to include or entertain children. If you have children who want to join in, get them drawing, cutting, and pasting alongside you. You can find additional coloring pages and activities for kids (or adults!) at the website interfaithfamilyjournal.com.

5. **Consult Resources.** At the end of the journal, and on the website interfaithfamily journal.com, you will find a list of books to help you better understand the landscape of religious and secular options around you, and to deepen your own interfaith education and that of your family members.

Can we make this more social?

This journal could inspire you to get a group of interfaith couples or families together to meet on a regular basis. You could create a journal group from several local interfaith couples. Or you could gather adults with young children (including single parents or grandparents raising grandchildren) who all want to think about how to approach interfaith education. Or, the group could be made up of empty-nesters who belong to the same church or temple, and are reevaluating what it means to be an interfaith family "after kids." In any of these configurations, it may work best if journal partners work through the chapters at home and then come together to have a group discussion and share some of the Get Creative projects they produced.

The group could meet just once, to celebrate together when everyone has completed the journal, or it could meet every week over six weeks so participants can support each other through the process. If the group includes children, consider assigning one or more adults to help entertain them in a separate room during adult discussion time; you can read stories from children's books listed in the Resources section at the back of this journal, or have them draw or color the downloadable coloring pages at interfaithfamilyjournal.com. After the adult discussion concludes, all ages could join back up to share some of the family recipes from Week Two, for a group potluck snack. If you're not up for cooking, try to get takeout representing the religions and cultures in your group.

Some of this work may be emotional or hard. You will be reliving your family's past, contemplating deeply held beliefs, and making decisions about the future. As an interfaith family, you will need to do this work, sooner or later, with or without a journal to guide the way. The journal, designed with input from hundreds of interfaith families, clergy, and counselors, simply provides a structure to help you through the process. By the end, you will have faced essential questions, listened closely to family members, spoken about what is most important to you, and created a plan for a joyful interfaith family. And you may find that through this process you have reached new religious, spiritual, or intellectual clarity.

Honoring Origins

I seek to speak to you, in some way, as your own self.
Who can tell what this may mean?
—Thomas Merton

Each of us brings our religious, spiritual, and cultural history to any new friendship, partnership, or family. Try thinking about the beliefs and practices you grew up with as wedding gifts, rather than as baggage. Do you need or want to display all of these gifts in your new home? Perhaps not. You might keep some in the attic and take them down occasionally, return or exchange some of them, put some aside for re-gifting, or even place some in the recycling bin. This chapter will help you to lay all your religious gifts out on the table, appreciate and honor those who gave them to you, and then lovingly consider how to sort through them.

Religious Ancestry

1-1.   What religious upbringing, education, and identities did your grandparents have? Did this change over the course of their lifetimes? If you have information on your great-grandparents, include that here too. If you are not sure about any of them, try to contact relatives and do some research on your family's religious history. If you were adopted, adoptive grandparents and great-grandparents may have played a formative role. If family religious heritage was not formative for you, because of emotional or physical separation, feel free to write instead about key religious or spiritual experiences with other beloved elders, such as friends or mentors.

1-2.   What religious upbringing, education, and identities did your parents (or mentors from your parents' generation) have? Did this change over the course of their lifetimes?

1-3.   How did your family decide how to raise you in terms of religious education and identity? Were they in agreement on this decision? If you're not sure, ask your parents or other family members how they made this decision.

1-4.   Growing up, what religious life-cycle events—such as baby welcoming, coming of age ceremony, marriage, or funeral—did you experience with family or close friends? How were these ceremonies meaningful to you?

Religion and Daily Life in Childhood

1-5.   Which houses of worship, if any, did you attend in your childhood and adolescence? How often did you attend and for how many years? How did you feel about those experiences? Which family members went with you, and how did you feel about that?

1-6. Describe any recurring religious practices in your home growing up. Did you pray or meditate together, or read from religious texts? When and where? At meals? At bedtime? What prayers were said? How did you feel when engaging in these practices as a child?

1-7. What religious objects were on display in your home (altars, ritual objects, religious artwork, framed calligraphy, religious texts)? What meaning did these objects or artwork have for you? How did you feel when contemplating these objects as a child?

1-8. What religious or cultural items of clothing, jewelry, or hairstyles did you and your family members wear when you were growing up? How did you feel about them?

1-9. Did your family eat foods associated with a particular ethnic or religious culture? What were they?

1-10. What music from your religious heritage did you listen to or learn as a child? Did you experience choral or instrumental performance as part of worship? Were you invited to participate in making music in a religious context? What was your response to these experiences?

1-11. If your family read to you (or later you read to yourself) children's literature telling stories from religious texts, or if your family told religious or cultural stories in an oral tradition, which stories made an impression on you and why?

Childhood Religious Holidays

1-12. What annual holidays did you celebrate as a child? Did you understand those celebrations as religious, cultural, secular, or some combination? How did these celebrations make you feel as a child?

1-13. Describe any worship services, home-based prayer or meditation, or specifically religious content of those holiday celebrations. What did the religious aspects of those holidays mean to you as a child? How did they make you feel?

1-14. Describe any special foods or meals associated with holiday celebrations in your childhood. Did you learn to prepare these foods or meals? Describe any other aspects of those holiday celebrations that you experienced as cultural rather than specifically religious (such as dress, decorations, games, gifts). What did those aspects mean to you? How did they make you feel?

Religious Education

1-15. Did you attend religious school as a child? If so, when, where, for how many years, and how many days/hours per week? What did you learn there, both socially and educationally? How did you feel about this religious school experience as a child? How do you feel about it now?

1-16. Did you attend a religion-based summer camp, or a youth or teen group as an adolescent or in college? Describe how you felt about that experience at the time and how you feel about it now.

Religious Mentors

1-17. What kind of interactions or relationships did you have with clergy members or other religious (or humanist) leaders as a child, adolescent, or adult? Describe how or whether these leaders supported you or your family. How did they express that support? What did it mean to you? Looking back, were your relationships with religious leaders stressful in any way?

1-18. Describe any family members (grandparents, aunts, uncles) who had a strong impact on your thinking about religion, culture, or spirituality. Describe any other friends, teachers, or mentors that influenced your thinking on religion. How did your thinking change after meeting them?

Religious/Spiritual Practices as an Adult

1-19. Since leaving your childhood home, list any religious/spiritual/humanist communities you have attended or explored. How long did you attend? If you left, explain why.

1-20. Describe any choices you have made about your current religious, spiritual, or nonreligious affiliation and/or identity. How did you reach those decisions?

1-21. How comfortable or uncomfortable are you with religious practices or in houses of worship?

1-22. Where and how often do you currently attend religious services or a humanist community? What do you see as the strengths and weaknesses of this community for you?

1-23. What religious or spiritual recurring home practices do you observe now (prayer, meditation, dietary observances)? What do they mean to you?

1-24. Are there religious or spiritual practices you do not currently observe, but that you would like to explore or that you intend to observe in the future?

1-25. What religious objects or artwork do you currently keep in your home, and what do they mean to you?

1-26. Do you currently wear articles of clothing, jewelry, or a hairstyle with religious or cultural significance? What do these mean to you?

1-27. As an adult, what annual religious holidays have you practiced in your own home? Why have you chosen to celebrate these holidays, and what do they mean to you?

Religious/Spiritual/Worldview Beliefs

1-28. How do you feel about the foundational texts of your religious heritage and/or current religion? Do you see them as sacred, as literal truth, as guidance, as metaphor, as literature, or a combination of these?

1-29. Whether or not you see these texts as sacred, do you think it is important to know stories or key phrases from these texts as a matter of cultural literacy? For your partner or children to have this literacy? Why or why not?

1-30. Are there parts of these texts you think are problematic or outdated? Why or how so? If so, do you think they should be taught with appropriate context and analysis, or excised and not taught? Should they be studied by children or only adults?

1-31. Do you see your religion(s) as part of the minority or part of the majority in the country where you live? In the region or neighborhood where you live? How does this affect the way you want to approach religion in your interfaith home?

1-32. Do you see all religions as equally true or valuable, or do you have a hierarchy in your mind in which some religions or worldviews are better than others? What do you think makes some better? How does this belief affect your relationship to the traditions in your interfaith home?

1-33. Is your religious heritage important to you for theological reasons? For cultural or historical reasons? For reasons of peoplehood or tribe? Or, not really at all?

1-34. Do you believe in God, or a god or spirit or other supernatural force in the world? What does that concept mean to you? Where is it found for you? Does it have different aspects? Do you understand God as listening to your prayers? Answering your prayers? Is this a God or spirit who can change what happens in the world? Why or why not?

1-35. Describe any other embodiments of God (including Jesus), spirits, prophets, saints, or gods and goddesses that are important in your life, and how you feel about them. Are there names or images of them in your home? What role do they play in your daily life or annual celebrations?

1-36. Do you believe in an afterlife? If so, describe the importance of this concept for you.

1-37. What motivates your desire to do good in the world?

HEARING EACH OTHER: INTERACTIVE EXERCISES

These exercises are designed to help you honor and respect what your partner has written. As you begin to engage with each other, it is important to maintain a nonjudgmental and "non-rebutting" frame of mind. In other words, try to simply listen rather than skipping ahead in your mind to rebut, refute, debate, or bargain with your partner. If you are working with more than one partner, it will take longer, but you can adapt all of the exercises in the journal to give each person a turn to speak, listen, read, and write responses.

Remain silent while your partner speaks, making sure to take turns talking and listening. This is not the moment for negotiating or deciding on compromises. This is a time for reassuring your partner that you are hearing them, learning from them, and working on how to gracefully receive and find a place for any gifts of belief, practice, and culture that they want to bring to your family.

1-E1. Find one line of prose or poetry from a sacred text, prayer, or secular source that had great meaning to you growing up, or in adulthood. Then sit across from each other (or in a tight circle of three or more), as closely as possible, in a quiet room where you will have an hour without interruption.

1-E2. Share the text you brought with your partner, and let them tell you how it resonates for them, or how they are wrestling with it. Talk about how you could continue to improve your interfaith literacy together.

1-E3. Now trade journals and read what your partner wrote about their childhood and adulthood practices and beliefs.

For exercises 1-E4 – 1-E8, you will each speak following each prompt. Take turns speaking first.

1-E4. Based on what you read in your partner's journal, make a list of the practices and traditions that you think were important to your partner growing up. Read the list to them, and then let them tell you what was most important, what you missed, and anything they forgot to write down.

1-E5. Make a list of the family members, friends, or mentors that were most important to your partner growing up. Read the list to them, and then let them tell you who was most important and why, anyone you missed, and anyone they forgot to include.

1-E6. Tell your partner what you now understand about how they feel about their religious education in childhood, adolescence, and college. Then, let them tell you what you may have missed or misunderstood.

1-E7. Tell your partner what you understand now about their current religious, spiritual, or secular beliefs. Name the concepts regarding their belief system that seem important to them, such as a monotheistic God, multiple gods or spirits, relying on other humans to change the world, prophets, the afterlife, or sacred texts. Then let them tell you what you may have missed or misunderstood.

1-E8. Tell your partner what you now understand about their current religious practices, holidays that are important to them, affiliation(s), and identity or identities. Then, let them tell you what you may have missed or misunderstood.

GET CREATIVE

Make a Religious Ancestry Tree or Garden

Creating a strong and successful interfaith family is an act of intention and creative visualization. If you see your family as having a unified trunk, and full branches bearing lush leaves and ripe fruit, you help to make it so. If you prefer to think of your family and other religious mentors as a garden, all growing side by side, rather than growing from a single trunk, you can use the garden image instead. Either way, creating art from these positive metaphors helps to dissipate any negative energy that may have been directed at your family in the past.

This project may be similar to a family tree you were asked to do in grade school. But this tree (or garden) will specifically illustrate the religious, spiritual, and/or secular identities in your ancestries. Another difference is that you are free to add tree branches or flowers representing mentors and friends who had a deep influence on you in terms of philosophy, religion, or culture, whether or not these folks are members of your family in the traditional sense. And finally, as an adult, both the process and the final product will probably mean more to you now than it did when you were a kid.

The best approach is to print out the photos, cut them out with scissors, and paste them with sticky dots onto a poster board to make a family photo collage. The process is engaging, small children can help, and the product can be a keepsake. If you are crafty or a scrapbooker, decorate the project to your heart's content! You can always take photos of the final product in order to create a digital version later. If you are more comfortable with Photoshop than with scissors, feel free to digitally cut and paste into a digital collage instead.

Materials

Family photos, felt, felt-tip pens, acid-free photo adhesive or sticky dots, poster board, scrapbooking materials, scissors, permanent markers, and wallpaper or cloth scraps

Step One: Gather information on the full names and religious affiliations of your parents, grandparents, and great-grandparents (or mentors) if you can, and/or your spiritual, religious, or worldview mentors. If you don't know the religious affiliations or full names of ancestors, contact relatives to try to collect this information. Create a text document with this full history for posterity. Note that many people don't end up with the same religious affiliation they were born into. Try to capture some of the complexity of each ancestor's consecutive or simultaneous religious affiliations. For example:

> Kimberly Harris
> Raised: Presbyterian
> Spent ten years also practicing Buddhism
> Died: Catholic

Step Two: Locate family photos of your parents, grandparents, and great-grandparents (or mentors) if you have them. Try to find photos of each person that fill the frame or focus on faces. Make sure to include a photo of yourself. Don't worry if you don't have photos of some of your ancestors; you can fill in their spots later with a drawing or just put text in their framed spot.

Step Three: Print out copies of all your photos. You want to end up with a photo of each person (preferably of their face) that is approximately the same size. If necessary, scan or take photos of old photos and print out copies on archival acid-free plain paper or archival photo paper. You want to end up with copies that you don't mind cutting up, so you'll need to copy any originals.

Step Four: Arrange the photos on the poster board in a combined interfaith family tree or garden. In a garden, the oldest generations could be the tallest flowers. Leave room by each photo for annotations. Cut away the backgrounds so that each photo is a portrait, perhaps in an oval portrait-frame shape.

Step Five: Using acid-free adhesive, stick the photos onto the project. Acid-free double-stick dots are safer and more secure than glue sticks. Under or beside each photo, annotate with names and religious affiliations. Try annotating lightly in pencil until you are sure everything is in the correct position. Then go over it with a permanent marker.

Step Six: Using permanent markers in different colors, draw leaf or flower shapes around the portraits and text blocks, and connect the leaves by drawing lines to indicate the branched relationships between the generations (if you're doing a tree). If you are inspired, you can draw a tree trunk and green outline around the crown of the tree. For a garden, draw a flower shape around each person and a stem growing from the grass.

Step Seven: Take a photo of the project so that it can be shared with relatives, children, or grandchildren, and so that the information isn't lost if you are tempted to throw out the poster board with a pile of old science fair projects! Stick a photo in this journal here:

WEEK TWO

Creating Home

All images once separate and alone,
Become the creatures of a tapestry.
—Adrienne Rich

You may hear voices—external and internal—asking you questions about your interfaith family. When are you going to make a clear and final decision about religion in your home? Are you going to commit to join a religious congregation, or decide not to? And what about the religious identity of your children?

This week, you are going to approach these questions from a different angle. Before even considering commitments, affiliations, and identities, imagine the sights and sounds and flavors, the hours of the day, and the cycle of the year in your interfaith family. Without worrying about labels or commitments for now, decide which religious, cultural, or secular practices you want to incorporate into your home life. What holidays do you envision celebrating together, and how? How can your family benefit from lifelong education about all the faiths represented in your home and heritage, regardless of the formal religious paths you take?

Together, you will create an inventory of dreams and desires, of practices you want to share with each other. And then next week, once you have described this vision to each other, you will look at the practical matter of local communities available to support you in thriving as an interfaith family, before making any big decisions.

Through this process, it is essential to remember that no decision is final in life. Each of us moves along a religious, spiritual, cultural, or secular trajectory that cannot be predicted. Life, illness, and death all happen. We meet new mentors and inspiring friends. We read, we experience, and often we move in new religious, spiritual, or secular directions. We can make decisions for our children, but from birth they have their own thoughts and experiences. As poet Khalil Gibran writes, "You may give them your love but not your thoughts, for they have their own thoughts." Our ability to determine their religious identities is confined to a narrow window of time, and perhaps even then may be illusory.

It may make sense for your interfaith family right now to choose a single religious affiliation, or dual affiliation, or no affiliation, based on your family's discernment process. But bear in mind that your own path may take a sharp turn, and in the future you may want to reconsider any promises you make today. We cannot force another person to hold to a promise of what they will believe, what they want to practice, which congregation feels most comfortable, or whether they want to attend any congregation, or practice any of these traditions in the future. As individuals in the complex interfaith family structure, we must remain flexible and empathetic, and remember that love comes first.

Daily Life

My husband comes from a family that includes some formal Protestant practitioners, and there are times when they expect to say grace before a family meal. I grew up Jewish, and a prayer "in Jesus' name" feels like it excludes me. My husband and I have taken to jumping in and offering to sing grace as a family when there's a call for a mealtime prayer. We have collected several simple blessings that work for those who aren't Christian, and even for those who don't believe in God. These blessings serve as a bridge between Christian family members who grew up with the ritual of saying grace at meals, those of other religions, and agnostic or atheist family members. Here's one of our favorites:

Thank you for this food,
This glorious, glorious food,
And the animals, and the vegetables, and the minerals that made it possible.

In this chapter, you will think about the religious, spiritual, or cultural practices you might incorporate in your home together on a daily or weekly basis. You will contemplate the foods, music, dress, and literature that you envision in your family life together. And you will imagine how you will support each other as you co-create new interfaith family traditions.

2-1.   What objects related to your religion and culture do you imagine having in your home together year-round? Religious artwork on the walls? Ritual objects hanging or displayed on shelves? Altars? Sacred books?

2-2. Would you want to enact rituals with these objects? Leave offerings of food? Light incense? Bless or touch the objects? Read from sacred books? How would you prefer that your journal partner and your children interact with you around these ritual acts? Give you privacy? Give you space and time and stand by respectfully? Join you? Learn how to perform these acts themselves when you are not there?

2-3. What, if any, prayers or meditations do you envision saying on a daily basis in your home together? Mealtime prayers? Bedtime prayers? Others? What prayers do you imagine would work best for your interfaith home? If you do say them, would you like your family members to say them with you? Stand by respectfully as you say them? Give you privacy to say them? Learn how to say them on their own when you are not there?

2-4. If your religious practice or family culture involves another language, would you like your partner and other family members to learn some of this language? How would you go about helping them to learn?

2-5. Do you envision wearing religious or cultural clothing or jewelry (including head coverings, modest attire covering arms or legs, religious undergarments)? Which ones, specifically? Would you want your partner or children dressing according to your religious or cultural customs? Would you want them wearing their hair and/or facial hair in ways that follow these customs? Do they have a way to learn about how to do so? How would you feel if they did follow these traditions, and how would you feel if they didn't?

2-6. Would you expect your partner and children to learn to sing or play music associated with your religion or culture? To listen to it? How would you help them learn this music? How would you feel if they did and how would you feel if they did not participate in or listen to this music?

2-7. Describe any foods or meals associated with your religion or culture you would want to eat on a daily basis. Who would cook them? Would you teach your family members to cook them? How would you feel if they acquired a taste for these foods or learned to make them, and how would you feel if they did not?

2-8. Do you intend to maintain any full-time dietary restrictions based on religious beliefs or cultural customs, such as refraining from alcohol, caffeine, pork, shellfish, or beef, or following a kosher, halal, vegetarian, or vegan diet? How do you envision your family accommodating these restrictions?

2-9. Do you envision starting or continuing to attend daily or weekly services or meetings at your current religious or secular community? Do you envision your partner or children coming with you? Do you envision attending your partner's community instead or as well? Alternatively, do you imagine finding a new community together? Ideally, what kind of community would that be?

Holidays

Holiday traditions often create some of our strongest formative religious or cultural experiences. Which holiday experiences feel essential to you, in terms of sharing them with your current and future family members? Which experiences could you put aside?

2-10. Make a list of the religious and secular holidays (weekly, monthly, or annual) that you celebrated growing up, or that you currently celebrate. After each one, briefly note whether you see marking this holiday in the future together as a) essential, b) somewhat important, c) possibly interesting but not essential, or d) not important. Think about why you marked each holiday as you did, and how you would explain this to your partner or other family members, including children.

2-11. Add to the list above any holidays that you have never celebrated, but would like to celebrate in the future with your family (this may be especially applicable for those who are affiliating with a new religion). How could you avoid misappropriating or misinterpreting these celebrations? Could you begin by celebrating with friends who grew up in this religion and culture?

2-12. Describe any foods or meals associated with your religion or culture that you would like to eat on holidays together. What would be some ways to teach your family to cook these foods together? How would you feel if they acquired a taste for these foods or learned to make them, and how would you feel if they didn't?

2-13. How do you envision your family accommodating the special holiday dietary restrictions or fasting periods that you want to continue to observe? Keep those foods out of the house and join you in your dietary restrictions or fasting when at home? Keep these foods in the house but ask family members not to consume them in front of you? Refrain from consuming them in front of you when you go out to eat? Ask them to commit to these holiday restrictions or fasting, whether or not you are with them?

2-14. Describe any particular pieces or types of holiday music you envision listening to, singing, or playing in your future together. Would you expect your partner and children to learn to sing or play this music? To listen to it? How would you help them to learn to do so? How would you feel if they listened to or participated in this music, and how would you feel if they didn't?

2-15. On which religious or secular holidays would you expect to exchange gifts in your household? When would you give gifts to children? When and how would you prefer that grandparents or other family members give gifts to your family?

2-16. Are there religious or cultural objects (decorations, lights, trees, ritual objects, clothing) specific to holidays that you would want to incorporate into your home holiday observance? List them here. Next to each object, note whether it has religious meaning for you, or whether it has a primarily secular or cultural meaning for you. (A holiday practice or object does not have to be religious to feel important.) Mark each object as a) essential, b) somewhat important, c) possibly not that important, or d) not important. Think about why you made your decision regarding each object, and how you would explain this to your partner and children.

Education

No matter how your interfaith family identifies or affiliates, every member of your family can benefit from lifelong interfaith education.

2-17. What can you personally commit to do to help educate your partner and children in one or more religious traditions or worldviews in your home? Read stories? Cook together? Teach songs? Teach a new alphabet or language? Teach prayers? Teach meditation? Discuss worldviews and philosophies and history? Teach how to celebrate holidays? What roles and responsibilities would each of you have?

2-18. Do you envision sending your children for formal religious or cultural education in a full-time school program? In an afterschool, Saturday, or Sunday school program? In a religious summer camp? Some combination of these? How would you work together to make decisions on formal religious education?

2-19. Do you envision sending your children for training or tutoring in preparation for a coming of age ceremony or for other religious purposes?

2-20. Have you discussed the costs (both in terms of time and finances) of religious or cultural or humanist school, afterschool, summer, camp, and tutoring programs with your partner and figured them into the family budget?

HEARING EACH OTHER: INTERACTIVE EXERCISES

Now it is time to read what your journal partner has written in this chapter, and reflect back to them what you understand about their dreams and desires. In this section, you will begin to imagine how to weave your religious, spiritual, and secular selves together into an interfaith family. But any decisions to follow specific religious paths may need to wait until you have gone through the questions and exercises in Week Three.

2-E1. Trade journals and read what your partner or family member has written.

2-E2. Gather some of the religious or cultural objects you would like to incorporate into your family together. These could be items of food, clothing, artwork, ritual objects, or holiday decorations. Place the objects on a table between you.

For 2-E3 – 2-E9, take turns so that each of you answers each question.

2-E3. Pick up each of the objects brought by your partner, and tell them what you know about that object, and what you think it means to your partner. Then let your partner remind you of anything you might have forgotten, or add details or family stories involving that object you might not have captured.

2-E4. Write a list of any daily or weekly religious practices that you think your partner would like to observe in your family together. These could be prayers at home; meditation; attendance at worship services; ways of eating or dressing; or religious imagery displayed at home. Then read this list to your partner and tell them your understanding of why each practice is important to them. Let your partner explain if they feel you have misunderstood anything or left something out.

2-E5.   Next, explain to your partner which of their daily or weekly practices you can see yourself participating in, even if you have different religious (or secular) beliefs. Would you go with them to worship services? Could you refrain from certain foods while at home? What religious imagery can you imagine having in your home?

2-E6.   For practices you feel you could not participate in directly, explain your feelings around these practices. You may feel intense discomfort around some of them, and it's important to help your partner understand why. Then think about and explain how you could still support your partner in their desire to continue with these practices. Could you care for children to give your partner time for these practices? Could you make physical space in your home for these practices even if you do not participate?

2-E7.   Talk to your partner about how it would feel for you to practice a religion (or humanism) on your own without your partner accompanying you or participating, if you are considering doing this. What would be the benefits and drawbacks? How could you meet your own needs and find support if you are going to be the only person in your family with this practice?

2-E8. Write a list of the annual religious/cultural holidays that your partner would like to celebrate. Read this list to your partner, and tell them your understanding of why each holiday is important to them. Let your partner explain if they feel you have misunderstood anything or left out an important holiday.

2-E9. Which annual practices still make you feel uncomfortable? Can you articulate why to your partner? Does your discomfort relate to theology? Or a lack of familiarity? Or a sense of loyalty to a minority religion? Or family dynamics?

2-E10. Tell your partner how you can imagine participating in these holidays, even if you maintain a different religious affiliation. Would you be willing to accompany your partner to celebrate these holidays elsewhere? Would you be willing to celebrate them in your interfaith home? Tell your partner how you feel about participating in these holidays, and discuss.

2-E11. Together, make a tentative calendar of holidays you will celebrate through the year together, marking each one with whether you will celebrate at home, with parents, with extended family, with friends, and/or in a formal community.

GET CREATIVE

When I was a young adult, my mother collected recipes from her own childhood and from my father's Jewish family as well, creating an interfaith cookbook without really intending to do so. One year, she spent many hours writing out four copies of this interfaith recipe collection, in a blank clothbound journal, one for each of her children. Now that she's gone, I treasure her handwriting in this little cookbook, which I still use. She left blank pages at the back, and I have collected additional family recipes there over time.

For this week's activity, create your own interfaith family cookbook, drawing on the cultures and holiday meals from all the branches of your new family. If you have young children, you can involve them in mixing and sampling as you test recipes. If they are old enough to draw, ask them to help illustrate the cookbook with pictures of fruits, vegetables, cookies, and cakes.

The result makes a great holiday gift for family, or an exceptional gift-bag item at a family reunion, baby welcoming, coming of age, or marriage. The cookbook works as a tangible and celebratory statement about your interfaith family as a source of joy. And it is a loving gesture to family members, who should be pleased to see their recipes included. It will certainly be a keepsake and heirloom.

Step One: Together, compile a list of your favorite dishes from each branch of the family. If you have older children, ask them to brainstorm with you, reminding you of their favorite holiday recipes. Remember that even families that do not have strong religious or ethnic traditions will still have special recipes for Thanksgiving or the Fourth of July, or everyday favorites.

Step Two: Ask family members who are expert in making these dishes to contribute their recipes. They can send recipes by email, or photograph written recipe cards and mail (or text or email) the photos to you. If the recipes have never been written down, ask permission to visit a relative and record the recipe as they cook.

Step Three: Gather the recipes and organize them according to seasons of the year, holiday themes, or type of dish (appetizers, main dishes, desserts, etc.). Including some of the recipe cards, if they are legible, in photo form preserves the handwriting and character of family members for future generations. Make sure each recipe is attributed to a family member and notes the relationship of that person to one of you. For example, "Recipe by Aimee Helen Rosenfelder, Susan Katz Miller's paternal grandmother." The relationships may seem obvious to you. But in another generation or two the cookbook may remain, while full names and the memory of the relationships can get lost over time.

Step Four: Add a note at the bottom of each recipe to identify when and how the dish was served in your family. Also note any information about the cultural, religious, or family origins of the dish. For example, "Martha always made this casserole on Christmas morning for her interfaith children and grandchildren." Or, "The Patels served this Gujarati dish every Thanksgiving in Minneapolis, alongside the turkey." Or, "This dish is served every Sunday in Brazil, and Paul learned how to make it during the years he lived there, from 1994 to 1997." Or, "Erica learned this Creole recipe from her Louisiana-born grandmother, Esther Brown. The okra ties this recipe to her West African ancestry."

Step Five: Invite children or adults in your family to create illustrations for the cookbook cover, or for each section, or even each recipe. Alternatively, you can include photos of family members with each or some of the recipes. Photos of family members cooking or seated at meals together work especially well. For the cover, you could use a photo of a group enjoying a festive meal together.

Step Six: Reproduce the cookbook for distribution to family members. If you are a scrapbooker or bookmaker, you might enjoy handcrafting a limited number of them. It works best to use a binding that will open easily for use in the kitchen, such as a spiral binding or three-ring binder. Plastic sleeves and indelible ink are also wise ideas: My mom did not realize that felt-tip writing will blur when splashed by broth!

Of course, these days it is almost irresistible to use one of the online services that allow you to upload and print a book. This approach lets you easily reproduce photos and illustrations, and create unlimited copies for purchase with a simple click. If you are uploading and printing, make ten extra copies, and save them for future grandchildren or nieces and nephews. You can also distribute your cookbook electronically, but the charm and permanence of a cookbook you can hold in your hand, whether handcrafted or printed on demand, can never get lost in a software update or hard-drive crash. On the other hand, if you are really inspired to go electronic, you could join a handful of bloggers who now have interfaith family recipe websites.

Finding Community

My destination is no longer a place, rather a new way of seeing.
—Marcel Proust

Now that you have done the hard work of sharing your religious ancestry, childhood experiences, current practices and beliefs, and dreams for the future, it's time to find support for your vision. The questions in this chapter are designed to help you imagine how you can find the communities that will work best for your interfaith family as it is today.

There is no one true path for all interfaith families—no single right way to create a successful interfaith family. The process of working through this journal will help you to match the way you envision your interfaith family with one or more of these available approaches or communities:

1.   **Choose one of your religions.** Together, you may decide that your family will practice just one of your religions. You will still need a plan for how to respect and honor the other family religion(s), and provide some interfaith education for children. This approach can work particularly well when one family member is alienated from their childhood religion and has no current religious affiliation. It can also work when both members of a couple, or co-parents, are passionate about religion, but one feels strongly attracted to another's religion and might eventually consider conversion.

2.   **Choose a new religion.** Together, you may decide on a new religious affiliation, one that neither of you grew up with, but that feels right for your life going forward together. Historically, interfaith families have found comfortable homes in religious traditions that emphasize unity and diversity rather than exclusivity, including Unitarian Universalism, Quakerism, Sufism, and Buddhism, among many other traditions.

3.   **Choose none.** Together, you may decide on a humanist or secular (freethinking) path, with or without affiliation with a humanist (or humanist-friendly) community that can fill many of the roles that were filled by religious communities in previous generations.

4.   **Choose both.** Together, you may decide to practice both (or more than two) religions represented in your backgrounds, with or without affiliation with a community (or communities) that will support you in providing interfaith education to the adults and children in your family. If a community does not exist in your area to support this option, you could create one. Choosing both can be a successful approach when both parents feel equally strongly about their own religions, or when each parent is somewhat nonreligious but wants religious literacy for their interfaith children.

5.   **Choose all.** Together, with each other and your children, you may decide to celebrate a wide variety of religions, from your own backgrounds and from around the world. Participating in a whole variety of communities will make it hard to feel strongly connected to each of them, but there are communities such as Unitarian Universalist or interspiritual communities that support families drawing on multiple religions. Or you could celebrate multiple religions at home.

You may feel pressure from clergy, family, or friends to choose the first option, picking just one religion for your interfaith family. Traditionally, religious institutions have promoted the idea that picking one religion is better for the children. However, there is no data to support this assertion, and families are moving away from religious institutions that insist on the "pick one" solution. For your family, picking one religion could be a successful approach, or another path could work better. The best arrangement for you will depend on what each of you brings to the relationship, what each of you wants for the future, and what kind of support you can find or build in your geographic area.

It is essential to consider all the options from the point of view of the adults (and older children, if you have them) working through this journal together. There is no way to completely ignore the opinions—whether solicited or unsolicited—that you will get from clergy, columnists, parents, grandparents, in-laws, and friends. But ultimately, it is you and any partner(s) and your children who will live in this family. Once you have been through four weeks of contemplation and discussion using this journal, you will communicate your ideas to family and friends with the help of the exercises in Week Five. Remember that it is your ability to be a successful family that is crucial here, not the institutional needs of a religious denomination or the happiness of a grandmother.

About those grandmothers. In my experience with hundreds of interfaith families, I find that even those grandmothers who feel they must make a dramatic stand on religion (such as refusing to attend a wedding) tend to come around when they spend time with our beloved partners and children. And religious institutions will need to adapt to the reality of sharing interfaith families rather than trying to corral them.

In order to come to an agreement on how you and your journal partner feel at this moment about your religious or secular path, the questions below are designed to help you imagine your own feelings, and your partner's feelings, in each of the possible approaches. Keep in mind that you are crafting a plan for how you feel in this moment together. That plan is not a binding agreement or an ultimatum. Five years from now, perhaps with children in the picture for the first time, or with children of an age to go to religious school for the first time, or with a realization or decision that you will not have children, your feelings about the religious practice in your family could change. And the feelings of your family members may change. At that point, you will want to take this journal out again, and run through these exercises again, to see where you stand together.

3-1. Imagine that your family chooses to practice your particular religion (or secular world-view) together. What do you think this decision will mean in terms of the holidays you will celebrate, your daily lives, your affiliation with religious institutions, and your children's education?

3-2. How does this hypothetical choice feel? What questions do you have? What more do you need to learn about your partner's religion to fully understand how you might feel? Describe the benefits and drawbacks of this path for you and your partner. How do you think your partner would feel about this choice?

3-3. Imagine that your family chooses your life partner's religion (or secular worldview) together. What do you think this decision will mean in terms of the holidays you will celebrate, your daily lives, your affiliation with religious institutions, and your children's education?

3-4. How does this hypothetical choice feel? What questions do you have? What more do you need to learn about your partner's religion to fully understand how you might feel? Describe the benefits and drawbacks of this path for you and your partner. How do you think your partner would feel about this choice?

3-5.   Is there a "third way"—a religious community new to both of you—that might work for your family? Have you looked into the "third way" traditions that have traditionally attracted interfaith families, including Unitarian Universalism, Society of Friends (Quakers), Sufism, or Buddhism? What more do you need to learn to consider this path? Describe the benefits and drawbacks of choosing a "third way." How do you feel, imagining this new path?

3-6. Imagine that your family chose to have a secular, humanist, and/or atheist household. What would that look like in terms of holiday celebrations, daily life, and the education of your children? How does this hypothetical choice feel? Would you want to affiliate with a humanist community such as an Ethical Society or Sunday Assembly?

3-7. Imagine that your family chose to continue to celebrate two (or more) religions, and educate your children in both (or all) of them. Describe the benefits and drawbacks of this path. How does this hypothetical choice feel?

66

3-8.   If you decide to celebrate both/all family religions, to what degree would you want to keep the religious traditions separate in time and space? Are you comfortable with mixing icons, such as hanging Hanukkah dreidels on a Christmas tree, or lighting a Pagan Yule log during Diwali? Or would you prefer to keep the celebrations and imagery separate?

3-9. Are there communities in your region designed by and for interfaith families practicing multiple religions? (See the Resources section below.) If not, would you be willing to help build a new community for interfaith families? Or would you prefer to try to find and join two separate communities (one from each religion) to support your family?

3-10. Are you interested in deciding to educate yourselves and your children about many religions, not just those in your ancestry? How do you imagine drawing from many religions? Are there interspiritual, multifaith, or Unitarian Universalist resources nearby that can support your exploration? Describe the benefits and drawbacks of this all-religions path for you. Describe the benefits and drawbacks for your partner and children.

HEARING EACH OTHER: INTERACTIVE EXERCISES

These exercises are designed to help you understand how your journal partner feels about the many options for your interfaith family. As your partner speaks to you, try not to refute or debate them in your mind. This is a time to listen deeply.

Next, you will work together to find the path that will work best for you together, here and now, knowing that you will always have the ability and right to make different decisions in the future.

3-E1. Sit across from each other, as closely as possible, in a quiet room where you will have an hour without interruption.

3-E2. If you like, place a bowl of water on a cloth on the table or floor between you. Together, dip your hands into the bowl to represent the idea that you are coming to this relationship refreshed and new and rinsed free of the accumulated disapproval and entrenched opinions of the institutions and family members that may have tried to lobby you on religious issues. Now, beneath the water, touch fingers to symbolize the idea that you will be building bridges between your experiences in a new and refreshing space that you will create together.

3-E3. Dry off your hands, and then trade journals. Read what your partner has written about the possible approaches to religious life.

3-E4. Tell your partner what you now understand about how they feel about these paths. Let them respond with any additional thoughts.

3-E5. Let your partner tell you what they now understand about your feelings about these paths. Then respond with any additional thoughts.

3-E6. Go through the list of interfaith family policies in various religious and secular communities in the Resources section at the end of this chapter. Discuss which ones you might like to explore together. Read the Get Creative section below now and use the hands-on project described there to help you search for communities.

3-E7. If you now agree on a particular path, it is time to find a local community or communities to support you. You may still feel undecided, unable to agree on a path together, or find that there is more than one path that could work for you. Sometimes a path will seem right on paper, but you cannot find a supportive local community associated with it. Or there may be a community that sounds like a stretch on paper, but thrills you in person. List the communities you intend to visit here.

3-E8. Read through the Get Creative section below, and then make a plan to visit each community on your list. Ideally, visit while the community is in session so you can observe and talk to other interfaith families there (many communities take a break or meet less often during the summer). You might want to call ahead and ask about their policies for interfaith families. For each community, it will be very helpful to get the answers to all of the questions listed below. Some questions may be answered on a community's website, but most will require talking with members or leaders from the community on a visit, or in follow-up meetings or phone calls.

3-E9. Keep notes on each visit. You will need to make a copy of the questions below for each community. Otherwise they may start to blend together if you visit more than two or three. If you like what you see and hear, it is important to follow up and meet with the leadership or clergy. They should be able to answer any of the questions below that you could not get answered on a more informal visit.

Questions to Ask About Each Community

- How do you feel about the language on the website? Does it feel inclusive and welcoming?

- How much is membership, tuition, expected donations, or tithing?

- How long is the commute?

- Is there specific programming for your family members (young couples, single parents, adults without children, babies, children, teens, seniors)?

- If you are considering being part of more than one community, how would that work, practically and logistically, with this community?

- If you are considering being part of more than one community, is the leadership (clergy, religious education director) okay with that, and do they understand why this might be important to your family?

- Do the clergy from this community perform interfaith marriages without conditions? Do they co-officiate with clergy from other religions? If not, how do you feel about that?

- Is there specific programming or are there groups for interfaith families? If not, is that okay with you?

- Is a spouse from another religion allowed on committees or in leadership? Can they participate equally in all rituals?

- Will your children be treated any differently because they have interfaith parentage, or because they are being raised in or educated in more than one religion? Will they be allowed to go through initiation (such as baptism) or coming of age rituals when they so choose, without conditions? Will there be pressure on them (or on either of you) to convert?

- Does this community apply religious labels to interfaith children based on the gender of the parents? How does the community welcome children who have the "wrong" parent from their religion? How do you feel about that?

- Did the clergy, other leaders, and community feel welcoming to you?

- How did you and your family feel about the space, service, sermons, and music?

- Is the community willing to match you with a mentor interfaith family in the community—in other words, to the people who are best equipped to act as guides and advisors in your experience in this community, and to help you to integrate?

GET CREATIVE

Materials

Corkboard, pushpins, paper, markers, and cloth scraps or other scrapbooking materials if you want to make a decorative border

Step One: Use a mapping application online to mark the addresses of all the potential communities you plan to visit.

Step Two: Print out the map in a large format, to cover at least two 8 ½" x 11" pages, if possible. Pin the map to the corkboard, and display it where you will see it frequently. Children can design and draw a border for the map, using religious imagery (crescent moon, six-pointed star, lotus, chalice, dove, tree) or any other design that inspires them.

Step Three: Put a colored pushpin in each site you plan to visit. If you are visiting more than one type of community, color-code them (for instance, blue for Buddhist temples, green for humanist communities, yellow for churches).

Step Four: Begin visiting communities. Remember to look for answers to the questions listed above. When you encounter a community that does not feel right for your family, remove the corresponding pushpin from the map. If you end up with one pushpin, you have found the community that fits you best, at least for now. If you end up with more than one pushpin on the board, visit each community a second time, making sure to talk to clergy and members in order to get answers to all the questions above. If you love more than one community, discuss whether there is one that makes the most sense for practical reasons (location, cost, programs, how often it meets). If you are drawn to more than one community and they represent different paths, discuss whether you want to belong to more than one community, and the benefits and drawbacks of joining more than one.

COMMUNITIES TO CONSIDER

You never know where you might find the right community for your interfaith family. A traditional Catholic, Hindu, Jewish, Muslim, or Protestant community in your area may happen to have warm and inviting clergy, an inclusive congregation, and policies that make your family feel welcome. Many interfaith families thrive in traditional religious communities. It is important not to necessarily judge an individual community by the official policies or historic traditions of that religion or denomination on the topic of interfaith families. Sometimes, a community or a specific clergy member will be far more welcoming and inclusive than you might expect after reading the official policies.

At the same time, it is important to be aware of the traditional policies on interfaith marriage and families, and to ask questions. And it is useful to learn about the various religious movements, denominations, and secular communities that have historically attracted interfaith families. Your family will choose to affiliate with one or more of these communities, or none, based on your own discernment process and the communities available to you geographically. Below are some brief notes on some of the choices you may be considering. There isn't enough room here for the thousands of individual indigenous religions, whether Native American or African or Asian, or all of the syncretic religions created through colonization, slavery, and migration. But some of these indigenous or hybridized religions very well may be good choices for your family, especially if they are part of your religious heritage.

Atheism, agnosticism, humanism. Remember that there are atheists in many traditional religious communities. While the dogma of a religion may be God-centric, almost any congregation may include atheists and agnostics who feel they fit there for the comfort of song and ritual, for intellectual stimulation, for social justice engagement, or simply to be part of a caring community. None of these benefits of community actually require a belief in God. But if you are in agreement, as a family, on wanting a congregational community that avoids God language, consider some of these options:

Ethical Culture. The Ethical Culture movement is one of the oldest humanist organizations in the Western world, with roots in the nineteenth century. Some of the founding members were Jewish, and Ethical Societies have always attracted interfaith families. Ethical Societies in at least twelve states provide many of the benefits of religious congregations, including regular meetings for adults, children's educational programs, and life-cycle ceremonies including coming of age programming. They also have an online community for those under age thirty-five. Go to aeu.org for more information.

Sunday Assembly. This new and fast-growing model from London is built on a Sunday-morning experience with singing, reflections, and comedy; it meets monthly. Described early on as "Atheist Church," it now has dozens of locations in the US and around the world and an easy template for creating new communities. It aims to be a "godless congregation that celebrates life" rather than promoting atheism. A similar model called Oasis Network meets weekly rather than monthly, and has a dozen communities, mostly in the American Midwest and South, and Canada.

Humanistic Judaism. See Judaism, below.

Humanistic Unitarian Universalist. A significant percentage of Unitarian Universalists (UUs) are humanists, and the Seven Principles of Unitarian Universalism do not mention God. Individual UU communities vary greatly in the degree to which they feel like a Christian church, mention Jesus, and use God language. But generally, they put great emphasis on making everyone, including atheists and interfaith families, feel comfortable. Generations of interfaith families and atheists have found a home in Unitarian Universalism. They may emphasize spirituality more than other atheist-friendly communities. UU theology often falls under the category of "religious humanism" as opposed to "secular humanism": It incorporates rituals of religious community, while believing that it is humans rather than God that create change in the world (the definition of humanism). You can read more at the UU Humanist Association website at huumanists.org.

Bahá'í. This is a relatively new religion, born in Iran in the late nineteenth century. It allows interfaith marriage, welcomes interfaith and interracial families, and has a universalist approach. Bahá'í teachings hold that Buddha, Moses, Jesus, and Muhammad are all important teachers pointing to the same God. Some interfaith families have found comfortable homes in Bahá'í communities. However, Bahá'í teaching (like Catholicism, Orthodox Judaism, and many traditional religious sects or denominations) rejects same-sex marriage, and expects LGBTQ individuals to remain celibate.

Buddhism. Many Americans and Asians practice Buddhism simultaneously with another religion. To some extent, they may see Buddhism as a spiritual practice rather than as a religion, since it does not emphasize creed or belief. Without getting into a philosophical debate about what constitutes religion, we can say that Buddhism welcomes interfaith families, and that individuals from interfaith families find it relatively easy to practice Buddhism alongside another family religion (including generations now of "BuJews"). Buddhist meditation communities are widespread in the US now.

Catholicism. Roman Catholic priests can marry Catholics to non-Catholics, though a Catholic will need a dispensation for "disparity of cult" if marrying someone who is not baptized. The Catholic spouse will be asked to promise to raise their children Catholic "to the best of their ability," but the other spouse is not asked to make promises. Catholic priests are allowed to work with other clergy at interfaith weddings, though not to formally co-officiate, and their individual willingness to do so varies. Some Catholic priests, notably in the Chicago area, have been tremendously supportive of families raising interfaith children in both Judaism and Catholicism, including priests who have participated in combined baptism/Hebrew naming ceremonies, First Communions, and bar/bat mitzvah ceremonies for these dual-faith children. Note that the various forms of Coptic Christian and Eastern Orthodox Churches may each have their own policies and range of responses to interfaith families.

Protestantism. Nationally and internationally, the mainline Protestant churches, including the United Church of Christ (Congregational), Presbyterian, Episcopalian, and others, are now very interested in welcoming families engaged in what Christian theologians are calling "multiple religious practice" or "multiple religious belonging." Most of these churches will be interested in learning about your family, supporting your family, and even learning from your family, whether you celebrate Protestant Christianity as your sole religion or celebrate dual religions. And many Protestant clergy members will be glad to officiate or co-officiate at life transition ceremonies.

Finding an evangelical church to support you may be harder. Many churches expect everyone in the family to be baptized and to accept Jesus as Lord and Savior, which requires a conversion, and so results in a conversionary family rather than an immediate interfaith family. (Although, remember that those who convert to any new religion will always be part of extended interfaith families.) Pressure to convert, or a belief that a family member is going to hell when they die, will make it very hard to have a successful interfaith family. However, there are also progressive evangelical churches now, so you would have to explore the churches available to you, and be careful not to make assumptions based on labels.

Jews for Jesus, or Messianic Jews, are evangelical Christian denominations in the sense that they require professing Jesus as the Savior, and work to convert people to this belief, even if they also encourage simultaneous Jewish ritual practice. Historically, they have evangelized to interfaith families, a practice distressing to Jews because of the long history of forced conversion of Jews to Christianity.

Hinduism (and other dharmic religions). The dharmic religions, including Hinduism, Jainism, Buddhism, and Sikhism, were all born in India, and share some practices, beliefs, and holidays. Generally, people of other religions are welcome to join in dharmic practices and visit these places of worship. The long colonial history in South Asia also means that many Hindus, Jains, and Sikhs are far more educated about Christianity than Christians are about dharmic religions. Partly because these Indian religions have strong ethnic/cultural components, they do not emphasize converting others the way belief-based religions such as Christianity and Islam sometimes do. But at the same time, because immigrant American adherents of dharmic religions may feel threatened by assimilation into the Christian majority in the US, some Hindu, Jain, or Sikh families may oppose interfaith marriage. (This will also sound familiar to people from Jewish families.) Interfaith marriage officiation by Hindu pandits is fairly common in the US, but strongly opposed in some other countries, often because of political tension between Hindus and Muslims. Sikhs have notably progressive philosophies of equality for all castes, and for women. However, they did officially forbid interfaith marriage in Sikh gurdwaras (houses of worship) relatively recently.

Interfaith Family Communities. In the 1980s, communities formed specifically by and for interfaith families celebrating both Judaism and Christianity began to crop up around the country. Currently, there are formal groups offering dual-faith Jewish and Christian education for children in Chicago (the-family-school.org), New York/New Jersey/Connecticut (interfaithcommunity.org), Philadelphia (iffp-philly.org), and Washington DC (iffp.net). You can read more on this grassroots movement in *Being Both: Embracing Two Religions in One Interfaith Family*. If you are interested in finding other families in your area celebrating more than one religion, and possibly creating new interfaith family communities, join the Network of Interfaith Family Groups on Facebook.

Islam. Traditionally, Muslim men have been allowed to marry "people of the book," including Jewish or Christian (but not Hindu) women. Muslim women, however, have traditionally been allowed to marry only Muslim men. And the tradition in many Muslim cultures has been that children of an interfaith marriage follow the religion of the father. (Note the contrast to Judaism, where traditionally children follow the religion of the mother.) Recently, some progressive imams and feminist Muslim women have challenged these gender-based standards, and supported Muslim women in interfaith marriages. Interfaith families may be drawn to Sufism (Islamic mysticism), which often has particularly open and inclusive practices. Islam is generally known for being open to all races and cultures rather than having an ethnic basis. Support for interfaith (and LGBTQI) Muslim families can be found through Muslims for Progressive Values (mpvusa .org), an LA-based network that has regular meet-up communities in sixteen locations. Muslim/ Christian Interfaith Families (MCIF) in the US can find each other on a new Facebook group.

And there are specific Muslim/Christian interfaith family support groups in England, Scotland, France, and Chicago, and online Muslim/Hindu interfaith family support groups in India and Indonesia.

Judaism. Here, we refer to the various Jewish individual movements, because, unlike most Protestant denominations, they have very clear, detailed, and distinct policies on interfaith marriage.

Orthodox. In general, Orthodox Judaism strongly opposes interfaith marriage and is not open to interfaith families joining its communities. It also holds strictly to the idea that Judaism passes down through the biological mother only.

Conservative. Conservative rabbis currently are not allowed to officiate interfaith weddings, though there is internal discussion on changing this policy. Children are considered Jewish only if their biological mother is Jewish. However, many Conservative communities now make a big effort to welcome interfaith families after the marriage. And a growing number of Conservative rabbis are pushing to allow interfaith marriages, or are leaving the movement because they want to perform them. Conservative Judaism typically includes a lot of Hebrew in worship, and longer and more formal services than the Jewish movements listed below. So the worship services may be less accessible for family members from other traditions, or they may appeal to them if they grew up with elaborate ritual in their own religion. Conservative communities are working on reaching out to and appreciating parents from other religions raising Jewish children. Children whose mothers are not Jewish will need to go through a conversion process if they want to be considered Conservative Jews. Conservative rabbis are generally willing to support this.

Reform. This is the largest Jewish movement in the US, and the most liberal of the "big three" regarding reinterpreting ancient Jewish law. Reform rabbis can make their own decisions about whether or not to officiate at interfaith weddings. Many do officiate, but they may apply restrictions. Many will not co-officiate with clergy from another religion, and some will ask you to promise to raise Jewish children. That said, many Reform congregations today actually have a majority of interfaith families. They may allow partners from other religions to serve on committees or teach in the religious school. Reform congregations are almost universally deeply appreciative of family members from other religions raising Jewish children. They consider interfaith children Jewish, independent of the gender of the Jewish parent, provided that the child is raised with Jewish rituals such as baby welcomings (bris for the boys) and b'nei mitzvah (coming of age).

Reconstructionist. This movement tends to be progressive on social issues (they broke ground on religious equality for women and LGBTQ people). Most recently, it became the largest movement to allow rabbinical students and the ordination of rabbis who are in interfaith marriages or relationships. Reconstructionist services tend to include more Hebrew and traditional liturgy than Reform congregations.

Renewal. This is sometimes considered the youngest Jewish movement. It aims to take the most progressive social justice ideas (including equality for women and LGBTQ people) and infuse them with the passion and music of the Hasidim (charismatic Orthodox groups such as Chabad). Renewal allows rabbinical students in interfaith relationships and marriages into their small rabbinic program, ALEPH.

Independent (or trans-movement or post-denominational). Some of the smaller rabbinical seminaries are post- or trans-denominational. Some of these rabbis go on to perform interfaith marriages. However, some of the best-known seminaries of this type (including Hebrew College outside Boston and the Academy for Jewish Religion in Los Angeles) still have policies barring rabbinical students who are in interfaith marriages.

Humanistic Judaism. This movement has never excluded rabbinical students with partners from other religions or backgrounds, has no bias in terms of which parent is Jewish, and strongly supports interfaith and intercultural families. Interfaith families make up a significant proportion of many Humanistic Jewish communities, raising kids with Jewish cultural knowledge, but without God-language. The Society for Humanistic Judaism lists twenty-six communities in seventeen states. If you are interested in this path but don't have a nearby community, the Society for Humanistic Judaism offers guidance on forming a new community, or being part of their online community on Facebook.

Other Jewish support. The national organization InterfaithFamily supports interfaith families celebrating Judaism (exclusively or alongside other religions) and keeps a list of Jewish clergy who will officiate, or in some cases co-officiate, at interfaith weddings and other life-cycle rituals (baby namings, funerals). They also train rabbis in major cities specifically to support interfaith families, and help them find local Jewish resources. Their website is filled with many resources and personal stories from interfaith families celebrating Judaism, including those who celebrate Judaism along with a second religion.

Interfaith families that are also multiracial may find community and support through explicitly multiracial Jewish organizations. B'chol L'shon (which means "in every tongue") and the Jewish Multiracial Network both embrace and promote Jewish diversity. Though neither organization has a specifically interfaith focus, they help families find information, events, or a community that supports Jewish diversity.

Unitarian Universalism. Unitarian Universalists (UUs) embrace spirituality without conforming to a specific religious creed, and draw on the texts and wisdom of the world's religions. It was formed by a merger of two earlier Protestant denominations: Unitarianism (as opposed to Trinitarianism) and Universalism (universal salvation and a focus on God's love). While no longer a Christian denomination, Unitarian Universalism in local congregations is still to some degree "culturally Christian." For example, worship typically occurs on Sunday morning, buildings are often called churches, and clergy are ministers.

For generations in the US, interfaith families have found comfortable homes in UU congregations. Jesus is recognized as a wise teacher rather than a savior, a sense of religiosity and full belonging does not depend on a belief in God, and children's religious education includes respectful inquiry into other religions. UU clergy often have expertise in life-cycle events in interfaith families (baby welcoming, marriage, coming of age, funerals). Unitarian Universalism allows for members to remain connected to different religious heritages, while also affiliating with an affirmative, liberal faith and a robust national and international religious structure. Nationally, there are UU organizations formed to advocate for and support UU Buddhists, UU Hindus, UU Humanists, UU Jews, UU Muslims, and UU Pagans, among others.

Marking Transitions

Love is the bridge between you and everything.
—Rumi

Even for those who have left religion behind, major life transitions including marriage, welcoming a baby, coming of age, and death may stimulate a return to comforting rituals, or a new spiritual search. Whether or not we share the traditional beliefs of a religious institution, we may find ancient practices, or the practices we grew up with, or practices that are new to us help us through these liminal moments. The liturgies and rituals for these transitional moments are among the things that religion does best.

You may be surprised when a spouse or co-parent who has long been nonreligious, nonpracticing, unaffiliated, or agnostic suddenly feels a desire to recite a prayer or enact a ritual or even return to a house of worship following the birth of a child or the death of a parent. To the extent that you anticipate and more deeply understand the meaning of these feelings, in yourself and other family members, you will be in a better position to help your family through these times of heightened joy and sorrow.

You may want to skip some of the sections below if they do not apply to you right now. For instance, you may not be considering marriage, or children, or a coming of age ceremony for your child or yourself. However, everyone should work through the section on death, since this is a life passage we all face, even if it seems remote to you right now.

Joining Lives Together

4-1.   If you are contemplating marriage (or a renewal of vows), where do you picture being married? Can you imagine and list any alternative locations?

4-2. If you want to draw from your religion(s) for the ceremony, what type of clergyperson do you imagine officiating? Are there particular clergy members whom you would like to invite to officiate? If so, list them. Can you imagine having co-officiants from two or more religions? If clergy are not available or desirable, can you imagine having a family member, friend, academic, or justice of the peace officiate? Or co-officiate? If so, list them.

4-3. If you prefer a secular service, do you imagine having an officiant such as a Humanistic rabbi, a Unitarian Universalist minister who does secular ceremonies, an Ethical Society leader, or a justice of the peace? Or would a friend or family member work better? List anyone who comes to mind.

4-4. List any songs, prayers, readings, or rituals that you imagine including in your service, and explain why they are significant to you.

New Life

4-5. If you are considering having or adopting children, what rituals or ceremonies do you imagine having to welcome them? Are there specific prayers, songs, ways of dressing the baby, foods served, or interactions with the baby you would like to incorporate? What do these rituals mean to you? What do you imagine they will mean to your children?

4-6.   How would you feel about a baby welcoming ceremony that draws on more than one religion or has co-officiants?

4-7.   If you already have children, what rituals or ceremonies were performed for them, and how did you feel about those rituals and ceremonies?

4-8.   If you have children who are no longer babies, what do you think about the idea that it is never "too late" to assign godparents or humanist mentors, or to create a ritual that connects a child to one or more religions or communities?

Coming of Age

4-9.   What coming of age rituals (for example, First Communion, confirmation, Hindu sacred thread ceremony, or bar/bat mitzvah) do you imagine your children having? What is the significance of these rituals for you? Which aspects are more important and which less? How do you imagine it would be similar to or different from the rituals that you experienced in your own adolescence?

4-10. How do you feel about the idea of an interfaith coming of age ceremony that would draw on more than one religion? Describe the benefits and drawbacks of this idea.

4-11. To what extent should children be allowed to choose to participate, or not, in any of these rituals? At what age? What do you see as the risks and benefits of getting the input of children on this?

4-12. What do you think about the idea that it is never too late for any of these rituals? Could they be done at age sixteen, or twenty-one, or seventy? If you have older children, have you discussed this idea with them?

When Life Ends

4-13.   For you, what are the most meaningful rituals around death from your own religion? Are there specific prayers, songs, ways of dressing, or behaving that have comforted you, or that you think might comfort you? When you die, do you imagine your family members enacting these rituals from your religion? How do you feel about that? How would they feel?

4-14. How do you feel about family members drawing on their own religions for comfort and meaning when you die?

4-15. At your funeral, do you imagine having a clergyperson from your own religion, or from your partner's religion, or co-officiants, or someone other than clergy officiating? List some people you can imagine fulfilling this role.

4-16. Do you wish to be cremated? If so, where would you like your ashes to go?

4-17. Do you wish to be buried? If so, do you imagine having an open casket at the funeral? Where do you want to be buried? Do you know the policies of the cemetery regarding interfaith families? Do you have a plot there?

4-18. What are the mourning rituals from your and your partner's tradition(s) for the first days, weeks, months, or year? Do you imagine participating in these rituals? Do you imagine your family participating in them?

4-19. What are your beliefs, whether drawn from your religion/culture or not, about the process of dying—including last rites, Do Not Resuscitate (DNR) orders, and assisted suicide?

HEARING EACH OTHER: INTERACTIVE EXERCISES

After trading journals, read the words of your partner with an open and non-rebutting mindset. Next, seek out some fresh air. Arrange a time to walk together outside, in a favorite park or garden, or in the wild, or even around the block in your neighborhood. Turn off your cell phones, and, if this is a romantic partner or dear friend, hold hands as you stroll. Think about the journey you are taking together, with all of the love, vows, births, and deaths you will encounter on the way.

4-E1.   As you walk, tell your partner what you have learned about how they see the role of religion in life transitions and the ceremonies that mark those transitions. What surprised you? What upset you, if anything? What moved you? Then, switch roles and let your partner do the same.

4-E2.   Tell your partner how you envision participating in some of the birth, marriage, coming of age, or death rituals from their tradition(s). Which ones speak to you? Which ones would you like to learn more about? Which ones make you feel uncomfortable, and why? Which ones would you like to experience, before deciding whether to incorporate them into your own family? Switch roles and let your partner do the same.

4-E3.   Discuss how you might help your families better understand each other when they meet at weddings, births, coming of age ceremonies, and funerals. (You will find more help with parents, in-laws, and other family members in the final chapter.) Consider getting together with each of your families separately to help them understand your interfaith family's life-cycle ceremonies. Think about planning a program for any upcoming ceremony with translations and transliterations, explanatory notes, and marked sources. Consider suggesting a few books from the Resource section or the website interfaithfamilyjournal.com to family members, in order to help them to feel more comfortable and get more out of any upcoming ceremony.

4-E4.   When talking to your partner about these life and death transitions, you make yourself vulnerable, and this is emotionally draining. If your journal partner is your romantic partner, this could be a good time for a silent bonding exercise: Sit across from each other in a wooded clearing or on a park bench or stoop. Get as close to each other as you can, and try gazing into each other's eyes without speaking for a full three minutes.

GET CREATIVE

For children, tell the story. If you have children who are three or older, tell them the story of their own welcoming to the world, whether that involved a religious ceremony, relatives coming for a first visit, a first stroll outdoors in a baby carrier, or other secular forms of celebration. Consider creating a simple scrapbook or digital photobook about the welcoming, with photos or illustrations. A child who is old enough, or older siblings, may want to draw a cover, or illustrations, or decorative borders.

If you did not assign godparents (or humanist mentors) for your children, consider improvising a brief ceremony to do it now. While the idea of godparents is a Christian concept, it benefits any child to feel a special connection to specific adults in the community, even if you are raising completely secular children. We did not designate godparents for our children when they were born, in part because it was not part of my Jewish upbringing. But years later, I decided to claim this Christian tradition for our family. We included our young children in choosing adults in their lives that they would like to have for godparents. We then explained to those adults what we had in mind (in our case, it meant someone who would be there for them and spend time with them occasionally; it didn't have anything to do with religious training). In one case, we had an informal "fairy godmothering" ceremony in our garden, with matching wisteria garlands we made from a vine growing in the yard, and short declarations of intent.

Adults, plan your own funeral. This may sound strange, depressing, or morbid. But it can actually be deeply satisfying to think of ways to be part of a celebration of your own life. Recently, a friend who knew he was dying wrote a letter, poignant and yet filled with his own brand of humor, that his widow read at the funeral. Those who attended were moved by the letter. Similarly, your family and friends may be comforted to know that you have thought about this moment, and that you have contributed words, selected music, or simply specified a favorite flower for your funeral.

As interfaith families, we may be called on to improvise, to create liturgies, and even to lead services. When my Episcopalian mother died, we had to figure out how to honor the religion she never formally left, while also honoring my Jewish father, the principal mourner. Having a rabbi lead the service didn't seem right, since my mother wasn't technically Jewish (though she raised four Jewish children). An Episcopal priest didn't seem right either, if only for my father's sake. And negotiating how a rabbi and a priest would pioneer some form of co-officiation seemed overwhelming in the moment, and like too much clergy. So I led the service myself, drawing on a lifetime of living in our three-generation interfaith family. It was hard, but also deeply satisfying to honor our interfaithness.

Your family members will be incredibly grateful if you leave them some clues about your wishes for your own funeral or memorial service. Especially in interfaith families, it is not always obvious what the "default" settings should be for these services, and bereaved family members will not necessarily feel up to trying to figure it out. Be sure to include your partner in the planning, since they will probably be a principal mourner. As you plan, think about how your family members may be feeling about religion and culture, and what they may be needing after you are gone. Remember, a funeral or memorial is more for the mourners than it is for the departed.

Step One: Get a folder that can be kept somewhere safe. Mark it clearly with "John's Funeral Plans" or "After Sarah's Death." Make sure more than one of your closest family members know where they can find this folder when needed.

Step Two: In a computer file or on paper, respond to the questions below. Trade responses with your partner, and discuss both plans. Print out your plan, and place it in the folder. You could also email it to one or more close family members for safekeeping. Even though you have just gone through some of these questions in this journal with your spouse or other immediate family members, it is important to record your wishes in a separate folder available to anyone who might need the information.

4-C1. Do you want to have a funeral or memorial? If so, how quickly after your death and where? Who might officiate?

4-C2. Do you want to have your remains cremated or buried in a cemetery, and in what location? Describe the type of casket (or organic alternative), if any, you would want. Include links or drawings to designs here, if you have them.

4-C3. Are there objects you would like to have buried or cremated with you? Items of clothing you would want to wear?

4-C4. List any favorite hymns or songs or live instrumental music you want included in a service.

4-C5. List any favorite prayers, poems, meditations, or readings you want included in a service. Print them out, and place them in the folder.

4-C6. Do you have favorite flowers, plants, or other decorative elements you would like to have included?

Reaching Out to Family

Be curious, not judgmental.
—Walt Whitman

Why did we save reaching out to your parents, in-laws, grandparents, and other family members for the very last week of this journal? You have spent the past four weeks contemplating your religious or secular past and future. You have exchanged intimate thoughts and dreams with your partner and developed a thoughtful plan for your interfaith family. Now you can visualize and articulate the boundary you have created together, a sacred or intentional circle, around this plan. You are prepared to stand together as an interfaith family, and support each other above all else, as you begin to articulate to others the path you have chosen.

Growing up, the experiences and conversations we have with our parents, grandparents, aunts, and uncles form us. The experiences and conversations we have with our chosen families (friends, teachers, mentors) can be equally important in terms of influencing our religious, spiritual, or cultural beliefs and practices. And often, all of these important people in our lives have opinions, whether subtle or passionate, about how we should live our lives in an interfaith relationship or family. You may need to make it clear to them that you are not asking for advice, but instead inviting them to be resources and part of your support network.

The task this week is to reassure friends and family that no matter which path your family is taking, you hear them and honor them, and still view them as important religious, spiritual, or cultural resources. You will invite them to be part of your support network, and explain how you would like them to respectfully share religious or cultural beliefs and practices. At the same time, you will communicate to them that you and your partner have made your own decisions about affiliations, education, and family practices. You will demonstrate to them that you stand together with your immediate interfaith family inside this new circle of love you have created, and that you are in charge of establishing and preserving its boundaries.

Reaching out to your closest family members (parents, grandparents, siblings) or closest mentors (friends, clergy, teachers) may not be easy if they have already expressed disappointment or disapproval about your interfaith relationship, or strong opinions about how your interfaith family should proceed. You may be guessing, or think you know, how they feel about your inter-faith family, or what is motivating their actions and statements. But guessing or assuming is not the same as engaging with them directly and listening deeply. The questions below are designed to help you interact with them in a constructive and positive manner. By reframing the conversation, you will reassure them that you do care about them and that you do respect their opinions and feelings, even if they are disappointed in the religious choices you have made.

Start With a Statement

If your journal partner is your romantic partner or co-parent, each of you will make a list of your own key family members or friends, and then, on your own, interview each of them. Before you begin each interview, it may be helpful to make a statement setting out your position and explaining why you are inviting them to play two parts—as a resource and teacher, and as a guest and student—in the religious or cultural life of your family. You do not have to announce a clear decision to affiliate with one or more religious communities, unless you feel inspired to do so. You may not have made a decision, or you may have decided not to affiliate but to have a home-based religious or cultural life. It's all good. And you get to decide what to disclose to others, and when.

In some families, these conversations will flow naturally. In others, or with certain relatives or friends, these conversations may be uncomfortable. Below is a suggested script for anyone who finds that helpful. Of course, feel free to use your own words, and of course edit this to fit your own family.

You will need to copy the questions below for each family member or mentor that you interview. Also, it will help to read ahead now to this week's Get Creative section, in case you want to visit relatives in person and combine the interview questions below with some of the activities in that section.

Write a list of relatives and mentors you need or want to interview. Be sure to include those who might be wrestling with your interfaith relationship.

SAMPLE SCRIPT

Hi Aunt Agatha. I really value your support and your role in our family as a keeper of traditions. So Sam and I wanted to let you know that we have decided, for now, that we will [*briefly describe where or if you plan to attend or affiliate, or how you plan to practice at home, or skip this sentence*]. We also wanted to let you know that we really respect your religious/cultural knowledge, and we believe our world will be a better place if all of us work on improving our religious literacy. So we want to invite you to help us as a teacher, to make sure that the important traditions in our family get passed down. And we also want to invite you to join our family in celebrating those traditions that Sam brings to our family, because this is a great opportunity for all of us to learn more about the rich religious and cultural diversity of the world. So we're wondering if we can come over to your place and brainstorm with you about ways you can support us in our new family.

Ask each of the people on your list the following questions, and record their answers.

5-1. What are the most important things you would want my immediate family members to know about your religious or cultural tradition or worldview?

5-2. In what ways do you envision sharing your traditions with these family members? Can you think of some family stories you would tell, songs you could teach, handcrafted projects you could make together, or traditional recipes you could cook together?

5-3. For which holidays could you imagine inviting my family into your home? Would you come to our house to learn about my partner's and/or children's holidays and celebrate with us?

5-4. Are there other things you are curious about and would like to learn about my partner's religious and cultural heritages or worldview?

5-5. Would you be willing to welcome my partner and/or our children to visit your congregation, house of worship, or secular group?

Explain that you need to speak to your partner and/or children and make sure that they feel comfortable with all of these generous offers of religious or cultural sharing. Promise to get back to them soon.

HEARING EACH OTHER: INTERACTIVE EXERCISES

After listening to your own family members and mentors, come back together, and process what you have heard.

5-E1. Take a blanket and spread it out somewhere large enough to lie down together (depending on your degree of intimacy with your partner): under a tree, on a beach, in a hammock, on a floor, or on a bed. Let this blanket symbolize the space you are creating together, separate from the world of opinionated family members, religious institutions, and friends who may or may not understand your interfaith family.

5-E2. Lie down side by side on the blanket, with your journal and family interview sheets on your chest. Realize that you are now inside this safe and sacred circle you have created together, and all your family members will need to respect the boundaries you have drawn.

5-E3. Trade interview sheets, and read what your partner's family and friends have said about how they would welcome you, how they could act as teachers, and what they would like to learn from you.

5-E4. Describe to your partner the ways in which you are inspired by what you have read. What are you excited to learn from your partner's friends and family? What are you excited to teach them? Then let your partner do the same.

5-E5. Using the schedule of holidays you began creating in Week Two, make a calendar, even if it is tentative and may change, marking which weekly or annual worship times or holidays you might spend with which of your various family members. Which holidays will you travel for? Which holidays could you host the family? Whom would you invite? Which holidays would you prefer to spend as an immediate family, or with friends instead of relatives? Keep in mind that you are bound to change your mind about some of these over time.

5-E6. If your journal partner is your life partner, now would be a good time to remind them that they come first for you, and that you will continue to communicate this to family and friends. Tell your partner what you are going to do to stand with them, and stand behind the decisions you have made together, even if family and friends continue to struggle with your choices.

5-E7. Report back to each of the family members or mentors you interviewed. Do this together, whether in person, by phone, or by Skype, so that the whole family gets the message that the two of you stand together. Let them know the ways that both of you welcome their offers to share religious and cultural practices with you, and to help in the religious and cultural education of your family. Let them know about any holidays you hope to spend with them. Be sure to express gratitude and excitement about specific plans, for instance, "Grandfather, Noah loves poetry. He can't wait to discuss Rumi and other Sufi poetry with you the next time we visit."

5-E8. At the same time, let them know if there are ways they can change the way they communicate about religious or cultural beliefs or practices, in order to respect the boundaries you have drawn. You may have to make clear statements such as, "Amina does not plan to convert, so we need you to respect that and not proselytize. However, she is excited about coming to Easter dinner at your house next week and learning how to make your hot cross buns." Try to end the conversation with a concrete plan for a positive moment of sharing culture or religion. For instance, "Can Sally come over next Sunday so that you can teach her how to wrap a sari in the Gujarati style? As a man, I can't really teach her that, and we would love to have your help."

GET CREATIVE

Step One: Plan a visit with a family elder or mentor (or more than one) to create a slideshow and oral history. Bring a digital recording device (which could be your phone), a notebook and pen, or a laptop to record family stories and history. Also bring a camera or a second phone to use as a camera. It will help to have two people (ideally, you and your journal partner): one to take photos and one to record stories. Read through all the steps below before going, in order to plan your visit.

Step Two: Before you arrive, ask your elder to gather some of their important religious or cultural objects: artwork, books, items of clothing, or handwritten recipes, and display them on a table. Also ask them to pull together photos of themselves as children, if they have them, especially any showing them engaged in religious holidays, rituals, or life transitions such as First Communion, coming of age rituals, confirmations, or weddings.

Step Three: Photograph each of the items and your elder holding or displaying some of them. Also, photograph or scan each of their photos.

Step Four: Each object or photo will probably elicit a story from your elder. Be ready to jot down, type, or record these stories as they arise. If your elder does not launch into stories right away, you can prompt them with the following questions:

5-C1. How do you use this religious object? What does this artwork depict? What does it mean to you? Where did you get it?

5-C2. Who is in this photo? What's happening in this photo? How do you remember feeling that day?

5-C3. Tell me about what your religion or heritage meant to you when you were a child.

A note on trauma:
Not every elder has happy memories associated with their religious or cultural tradition. Almost every family, at some point in history, has experienced war and displacement or poverty due to religious intolerance. Many had to flee to a new country, or suffered cultural oppression, internment, enslavement, forced displacement, or genocide based on race, ethnicity, culture, or religion. Recently, scientists have ventured into a whole new field, epigenetics, exploring how trauma such as genocide or slavery actually becomes encoded in our genes and is passed down to subsequent generations.

These heavy stories become a part of our religious and cultural heritage that may at times overshadow any positive memories of food, song, and community. Some elders feel called on to pass down these stories of trauma so that families will never forget them. Others may not want to return to thinking about traumatic times. All you can do is indicate your sincere desire to hear and record the stories, both the joyful and the painful ones, and let your elder decide which ones to tell.

Step Five: Don't forget to take a portrait of your elder. And don't forget to take a selfie with your elder (or ask your partner in this project to take a portrait of you together).

Step Six: If you can, put together a digital slideshow of the photos you have captured. You then have several options:

- Create a soundtrack of your elder's voice telling family stories and explaining the photos and objects.

- Insert text slides with brief versions of the stories, explaining the objects and photos, so that they're preserved in a visual format.

- Narrate the slideshow yourself when you show the photos, telling the stories you have learned.

- Have your elder serve as the narrator, as you show the slides.

Step Seven: Return to show your elder the slideshow in person, and then show it at the next family gathering. Make sure you have it saved in multiple ways (in the cloud, on a hard disk, and printed out) so that others, including any descendants, can learn from it in the future.

GOING FORWARD

As time goes by, you will experience marriages, births, illnesses, and deaths. And you will certainly experience the everyday joys and concerns of work, relationships, and the world. It is useful to think about how the religious affiliations, communities, and practices you have chosen are meeting your needs. Are you getting casseroles if you need them in times of trouble? Are you getting the spiritual and intellectual nourishment you desire? In response to life transitions, or simply because of your experience of daily living, you may occasionally want to revisit your ideas about belief, practice, and tradition.

Also, you many notice changes in the beliefs and practices of your life partner or children. Clergy may come and go in your community or communities. Congregations you belong to may change over time. New communities may spring up around you. You may feel drawn to new beliefs and practices, based on your own reading, friendships, or teachers. For all or any of these reasons, you may reevaluate your earlier decisions about how your interfaith family celebrates together, and where or if your family chooses to affiliate.

This is the moment to pull out this journal again. Reread your responses, and think about changes you would make to your answers. Have your original journal partner (or a new partner) do the same. And if you have children who are tweens or teens now, invite them to record their own answers to the questions in Weeks One through Three. You might consider giving them their own copies of this journal, as an acknowledgement of the importance of their role in family decision-making.

Next, review how everyone in the family now feels. Have your beliefs changed? Your partner's beliefs? If you have older children, what is their developing sense of personal theology? What religious, spiritual, or cultural practices speak to them? Are they claiming specific identity labels for themselves?

In a family conversation, discuss whether you want to shift the way your family identifies, the congregations you join, or the communities you claim. Keep in mind that it is never too late to join a religious or secular community, to claim religious or cultural heritage, or to add (or subtract) new practices and holidays to your family life. You might need to go through the Get Creative section in Week Three again to determine which communities are available to you in your geographic area. If you are (re)visiting communities, be sure to take your children with you so that they can be part of the decision.

Finally, go over the responses that you and your journal partner gave on life transitions in Week Four. Have you changed the way you envision marking the transitions in your own life and the life of your family? Remember that it is never too late to welcome a child, to assign godparents, to renew your marriage vows, to "come of age" in a religious community with a ceremony such as a baptism or bar/bat mitzvah, or to change how you plan to honor the deaths in your family.

Some interfaith families find a path that continues working for them over a lifetime, or even over generations. Others will be flexible and fluid, making subtle adjustments to the plan, or steering into a new lane entirely, once or more than once. The process of discerning a successful path for your family can be a form of lifelong spiritual or intellectual work. You may feel enlightened, inspired, and uplifted by navigating the complex architecture of your spiritual, religious, or cultural traditions. Getting to understand the surprising ways in which these traditions may overlap or grow from each other, or push against each other, can foster affection for the unique and particular interfaith family structure you are building together.

Cultivating love and pride for the interfaith home you are envisioning together will help you to become interfaith ambassadors. You are demonstrating to family, friends, and the rest of our troubled world how love can bridge divides, and vault across barriers. As an interfaith family, you are creating peace—day by day, year in and year out—as you connect communities and ideas and cultures. No matter which path you are on, your persistence and creativity in wrestling with how to be the best interfaith family you can be will send out a message of hope.

RESOURCES

Pluralism and Interfaith History

American Grace: How Religion Divides and Unites Us, Robert D. Putnam and David E. Campbell. Simon & Schuster, 2012. A lively academic account of the complexity of the American religious landscape.

The End of White Christian America, Robert P. Jones. Simon & Schuster, 2016. How white Christians are responding to becoming a minority in America.

A History of God: The 4,000 Year Quest of Judaism, Christianity and Islam, Karen Armstrong. Ballantine Books, 1994. Acclaimed popular religious history text.

Interfaith Leadership: A Primer, Eboo Patel. Beacon Press, 2016. The Muslim leader of a national interfaith engagement program for college students on the skills needed for interfaith leadership.

A New Religious America: How a "Christian Country" Has Become the World's Most Religiously Diverse Nation, Diana L. Eck. HarperSanFrancisco, 2002. A religious studies scholar on the changing American religious landscape.

When One Religion Isn't Enough: The Lives of Spiritually Fluid People, Duane Bidwell. Beacon Press, 2018. A theology professor who is both Buddhist and Christian interviews people who practice more than one religion.

The World's Religions, Huston Smith. HarperOne, 2009. The classic survey text on the world's religions, still used in many college classrooms.

Interfaith Families

Being Both: Embracing Two Religions in One Interfaith Family, Susan Katz Miller. Beacon Press, 2013. Journalistic account of the national movement to provide interfaith children with dual-faith education.

Beyond Chrismukkah: The Christian-Jewish Interfaith Family in the United States, Samira K. Mehta. University of North Carolina Press, 2018. An academic provides a helpful review of interfaith families in popular culture and different interfaith family paths.

Celebrating Our Differences: Living Two Faiths in One Marriage, Stanley Ned Rosenbaum and Mary Helene Rosenbaum. Ragged Edge Press, 1998. A Jew and a Catholic write a witty and groundbreaking account of raising children with both religions.

Common Prayers: Faith, Family, and a Christian's Journey Through the Jewish Year, Harvey Cox. Mariner Books, 2002. Specifically for Christian parents raising Jewish children.

In Faith and In Doubt: How Religious Believers and Nonbelievers Can Create Strong Marriages and Loving Families, Dale McGowan. AMACOM, 2014. How atheists and religious believers (including evangelical Christians) can have successful families.

Interfaith Marriage in America: The Transformation of Religion and Christianity, Erika B. Seamon. Palgrave Macmillan, 2012. A lively academic history of how Christianity has approached interfaith marriage through the ages.

Marrying Out: Jewish Men, Intermarriage, and Fatherhood, Keren McGinity. Indiana University Press, 2014. An academic defense of Jewish men in interfaith relationships raising Jewish children.

Our Haggadah: Uniting Traditions for Interfaith Families, Cokie and Steve Roberts. HarperCollins, 2011. A practical guide for interfaith families, whether they are celebrating their first Passover or are starting a new tradition.

Raising Your Jewish/Christian Child: How Interfaith Parents Can Give Children the Best of Both Their Heritages, 2nd edition, Lee Gruzen. William Morrow, 2001. By a founder of New York's Interfaith Community, the first group to provide dual-faith education for interfaith children.

Saffron Cross: The Unlikely Story of How a Christian Minister Married a Hindu Monk, J. Dana Trent. Fresh Air Books: 2013. A memoir by a Baptist minister on a steep learning curve about her partner's Hinduism.

Strange Wives: The Paradox of Biblical Intermarriage, Stanley Ned Rosenbaum and Rabbi Allen Secher. Edited and published by Mary Rosenbaum, 2014. A Jewish Studies scholar and a rabbi in conversation on the history of interfaith marriage in biblical times.

For Children

The list below includes primarily Christian, Hindu, Jewish, and Muslim children's books. For a more extensive and inclusive list, go to interfaithfamilyjournal.com.

Aisha's Moonlit Walk, Anika Stafford. Skinner House, 2005. PreK–3. A family celebrates eight pagan holidays through the cycle of the year.

All-of-a-Kind Family, Sydney Taylor. Yearling, 1984. Grades 3–7. First in a beloved series of chapter books about a Jewish family in New York at the beginning of the twentieth century.

Amma, Tell Me About Diwali!, Bhakti Mathur. Anjana, 2011. PreK–3. One in a series on various aspects of Hinduism.

Ayat Jamilah: Beautiful Signs: A Treasury of Islamic Wisdom for Children and Parents, Sarah Conover and Freda Crane. Skinner House, 2010. K and up. Includes stories from cultures throughout the Muslim world.

Beni's Family Treasury: Stories for the Jewish Holidays, Jane Breskin Zalben. Henry Holt and Company, 1998. Grades K–3. One of a dozen books (five collected here) with animal families celebrating holidays, and life-cycle events. Out of print: worth seeking out.

Children of God Storybook Bible, Desmond Tutu. Zondervan: 2010. Archbishop Tutu retells more than fifty of his most beloved Bible stories, artfully highlighting God's desire for all people to love one another and to find peace and forgiveness in their hearts. Grades PreK–3.

December's Gift: An Interfaith Holiday Story, Ashley Smith-Santos and Stasie Bitton. Stasie Bitton, 2012. K–3. An interfaith child celebrates both Christmas and Hanukkah.

Eight Candles and a Tree, Simone Bloom Nathan. Beaver's Pond Press, 2014. PreK–2. An interfaith child celebrates both Christmas and Hanukkah.

Images of God for Young Children, Marie-Helene Delval. Eerdmans: 2010. Explains the concept of God to children in creative, often metaphorical ways. Many of the characteristics of God are commonly discussed in Christian settings, such as viewing God as a shepherd, healer, or parent. Other images of God are unusual, presenting God as silence or joy or in our tears. Grades K–4.

It's Ramadan, Curious George, H.A. Rey and Hena Khan. HMH Books, 2016. Boardbook. The mischievous monkey celebrates the Muslim holidays of Ramadan and Eid.

Jalapeño Bagels, Natasha Wing. Atheneum, 1996. K–3. The story of a boy with a Mexican parent and an Ashkenazi Jewish parent, with Spanish and Yiddish.

Kindness: A Treasury of Buddhist Wisdom for Children and Parents, Sarah Conover and Valerie Wahl. Skinner House, 2010. K and up. Stories from throughout the Buddhist world.

Lailah's Lunchbox: A Ramadan Story, Reem Faruqi. Tilbury House, 2015. Grades 1–7. A young Muslim girl wrestles with being a Muslim, and how to fast, while at school.

The Little Book of Hindu Deities: From the Goddess of Wealth to the Sacred Cow, Sanjay Patel. Plume, 2006. PreK and up. Lively cartoon images and child-friendly stories.

Lola Levine is Not Mean!, Monica Brown and Angela Dominguez. Little, Brown, 2015. Grades 1–5. First in a series of chapter books featuring a girl with one Ashkenazi Jewish parent and one Peruvian-Catholic parent.

Meet Jesus: The Life and Lessons of a Beloved Teacher, Lynn Tuttle Gunney. Skinner House, 2007. Beautiful illustrations and a simple text follow the life of Jesus. Grades PreK–3.

Mrs. Katz and Tush, Patricia Polacco. Dragonfly, 1994. Grades K–3. One of several classics by Polacco about friends of different religions: in this case, an elderly Jewish immigrant and a young African American boy.

The Mystic Bible, Alexandra Sangster. Sophia Books: 2012. Journeys with Jesus from his birth through to the Pentecost experience and invites children to explore the sacred stories from a contemporary perspective. Vivid illustrations; uses inclusive language and images. All ages.

Night of the Moon: A Muslim Holiday Story, Hena Khan. Chronicle, 2008. PreK–3. A picture book on Ramadan and Eid.

Nonna's Hanukkah Surprise, Karen Fisman. Kar-Ben, 2013. PreK–3. An interfaith child being raised Jewish celebrates Hanukkah with her Christian grandmother.

Queen of the Hanukkah Dosas, Pamela Ehrenberg. Farrar, Straus, and Giroux, 2017. Grades K–2. A family with an Indian mom (no mention of her religion) and Jewish dad celebrates Hanukkah with South Indian foods.

Ramayana: Divine Loophole, Sanjay Patel. Chronicle, 2010. K and up. Based on the classic Hindu text, with rich contemporary illustrations by a Pixar animator.

Sammy Spider's First Hanukkah, Sylvia Rouss. Kar-Ben, 1993. Grades K–2. First in a series of books on various Jewish holidays.

Stories Jesus Told, Nick Butterworth. Multnomah: 1994. Retells eight parables that help draw young Christians closer to God. Grades PreK–2.

Under the Ramadan Moon, Sylvia Whitman. Albert Whitman and Company, 2008. PreK–2. A picture book on a contemporary family celebrating Ramadan.

Ved and Friends Celebrate Dussehra and Diwali, Diksha Pal Narayan. Small Town Publishing, 2017. A group of friends from multiple South Asian religious traditions share their celebrations.

Yo Soy Muslim: A Father's Letter to His Daughter, Mark Gonzalez. Simon and Schuster, 2017. PreK–3. A letter by a Muslim and Latino poet to his child.

Life Cycle

Birth

Bless This Child: A Comprehensive Guide to Creating Baby Blessing Ceremonies, Susanna Stefanachi Macomb. iUniverse, 2011. Draws on many religions.

Making Our Way to Shore: A Celebration of Hebrew Naming and Baptism, Eileen O'Farrell Smith. Virtualbookworm.com, 2004. Specifically for Catholic/Jewish interfaith families celebrating both, includes description of combined ceremonies, and interviews with clergy about how this works.

Marriage

Interfaith Wedding Ceremonies: Samples and Sources, Joan C. Hawxhurst. Dovetail Publishing, 1996. Includes sample Christian/Jewish ceremonies. By the founder of an organization that supported all interfaith families, no matter which path they chose.

Joining Hands and Hearts: Interfaith, Intercultural Wedding Celebrations: A Practical Guide for Couples, Susanna Macomb with Andrea Thompson. Atria Books, 2003. An interfaith/interspiritual minister draws on her extensive experience with Christian, Jewish, Muslim, Hindu, and secular interfaith couples.

The Perfect Stranger's Guide to Wedding Ceremonies: A Guide to Etiquette in Other People's Religious Ceremonies, Stuart Matlins (editor). Skylight Paths, 2000. Covers etiquette and what to expect at weddings in thirty religions and denominations.

We Pledge Our Hearts: A Treasury of Poems, Quotations, and Readings to Celebrate Love and Marriage, Edward Searl. Skinner House, 2005. A Unitarian Universalist minister draws from ancient and modern sources.

Death

Beyond Absence: A Treasury of Poems, Quotations, and Readings on Death and Remembrance, Edward Searl. Skinner House, 2005. Helpful for funeral or memorial planning of any religions or none, from a Unitarian Universalist minister.

In Memoriam: A Guide to Modern Funeral and Memorial Services, Edward Searl. Skinner House, 2000. A Unitarian Universalist minister writes a practical guide to planning, along with sample services.

The Perfect Stranger's Guide to Funerals and Grieving Practices: A Guide to Etiquette in Other People's Religious Ceremonies, Stuart Matlins (editor). SkyLight Paths, 2000. Description of funeral practices in thirty-eight religions and denominations.

Remembering Well: Rituals for Celebrating Life and Mourning Death, Sarah York. Apollo Ranch Institute Press, 2012. A Unitarian Universalist minister offers practical advice for planning memorials and processing grief, including a chapter on interfaith families.